"THIS IS A BOOK EVERY WOMAN SHOULD READ...

... Lumb is a master at presenting financial information which is understandable to the beginner, yet interesting and useful also to those 'in the know.' "
—Didi Furman Scott, Allied Publications

"Will serve as a valuable tool . . . in establishing your own personal objectives. Heed his advice now and your good intentions won't be someone else's example of 'too late, too bad!' "
—Peggy Jessup, C.P.A.

"Lumb's book is extremely well-timed. Now that women are more business-oriented, we need expert advice in the financial planning area. This is the most comprehensive book of its kind I have ever read, and I urge every woman to read it and keep it as a permanent reference."
—Betty Groff, Director,
Nationwide Insurance Corporation

A popular author and lecturer, *Fred A. Lumb* has more than forty years of experience as a trusted and expert consultant on financial affairs.

WHAT EVERY WOMAN
SHOULD KNOW ABOUT FINANCES

Fred A. Lumb

A BERKLEY BOOK
published by
BERKLEY PUBLISHING CORPORATION

BERKLEY BOOKS are published by
Berkley Publishing Corporation
200 Madison Avenue
New York, N.Y. 10016

BERKLEY BOOK® TM 757,375

Printed in the United States of America

Berkley Edition, MARCH, 1979

To

Four very special women in my life:

Cally, Marilyn, Carol, and Janet —
wife, daughters, and granddaughter.

ACKNOWLEDGMENTS

Fairness requires that I express appreciation to scores of clients whom I have served over the years. These are people from whom I have learned much, and who provided most of the examples in this book.

Then there are many, many colleagues with whom I have worked in various parts of the country. These attorneys, accountants, life underwriters, and trust officers have been not only helpful, but also, with few exceptions, cooperative and competent. In those rare instances in which our judgments differed, the give-and-take of our opinions invariably was tempered by the mutual aim of serving the client's best interests, and by our mutual respect. I am grateful for many firm friendships which have matured from these associations.

Each chapter of this book has been scrutinized by an expert in the subject matter of the particular chapter. An accountant, an attorney, two persons who head their own successful and long established businesses, and four corporate executives, all at vice presidential level or higher, make up the group. Their suggestions have been most helpful.

Finally, I am indebted to Dr. Gordon Q. Freeman

for her continuing appraisal of copy as the manuscript was being written, to make sure that it remained in keeping with "the woman's viewpoint," and to Ms. Phyllis Byrnes for her interested help in preparing the final draft of the book.

ABOUT THE AUTHOR

When we first talked with Fred Lumb about publishing this book we quickly became convinced of the real need among women for the sort of material it contains. He writes about that in the Introduction.

What is even more important, he has an unique background of qualifications.

He has been involved in estate and financial planning work as a practitioner for many years. He is not a theoretician. He has worked closely with attorneys, insurance persons, trust officers, and CPA's and, of course, with scores and scores and individual clients.

He has served as vice-president of a major life insurance company and, following retirement, was a vice-president for trust marketing services, including estate planning services, for a sizable trust company.

Fred Lumb continues to be in demand as a speaker and as a conductor of seminars. He remains active as a consultant and as a writer.

Already the author of four books, he knows how to write lucidly and in an easy-to-read style. True-life examples brighten the pages.

More than helpful, this book is interesting from the simple basics at the beginning to the more complex subjects of the last few chapters. You will find yourself wanting to read on.

THE PUBLISHER

Contents

Introduction

The professor who taught my freshman Survey of English Literature course made a statement which is appropriate at the outset of this book. This is what she said: "People are more interested in those subjects about which they know something."

In forty years of experience with financial and estate planning matters, I have observed that one of the great concerns of women is that of proper understanding and arrangement of these affairs.

I think not so much of a couple of extreme cases I have known in which recent widows had never been taught how properly to write checks or keep a checkbook, as I do of a statement made to me not long ago by a competent career woman, an executive. She said, "I don't know a fraction of what I should regarding finances."

This book is not essentially for the "pros," though it may serve them as a reminder of some basics which easily are forgotten after years of working with complicated cases. It is rather for that great number of women whose knowledge of financial and estate planning matters falls somewhere between little and quite a bit.

To go back to my professor's statement—if what you read herein enables you to "know something" more than you know now, then undoubtedly you will become "more interested" in the subject—an end wisely to be desired in these changing and economically troubled times.

                                        F.A.L.

I
Some Ground Rules

Objectives—Necessary Information—Professional Guidance—Funds and Functions—Certainty of Change

Making a Start

Time after time women have said to me that they want to know what I think about investing in this or that, or about changing the nature of property ownership, or about buying this or that kind or amount of insurance, or about one move or another in their financial arrangements.

Then I ask, "Why?"

Puzzled, they look at me and say, "What do you mean by 'Why'?"

"Why are you thinking of doing that?" I respond.

Never have I received the answer, "Because it seems to fit in with my total planning." Much more likely the answer has been:

"I read about it in the newspaper."
or
"My neighbor told me about it, and I thought it sounded like a good idea."
or
"I don't know. I have this money (or a nice raise) coming to me, and I have to do something with it."

None of which is a very good reason. None was designed to achieve specific short or long-term objectives. After objectives were analyzed the proposed action may or may not have been taken. But whatever was done was done for a reason which was predicated upon aim rather than aimlessness.

Here is a personal example. For many years I bought and sold investments on the basis of their providing some income, but much more on the basis of growth possibilities. (As you will see in the next chapter this means a lower rate of return.) I did not need the income, and even if I had it I would have had to pay a fairly high income tax on it. The possibilities of gain from growth were attractive, and the chances of loss were acceptable.

I had long planned that at a certain time in my career I would shift the emphasis to income. When that time came I began the transition. The result is that today the rate of return is about double what it used to be, but the likelihood of growth is much less.

That does not prove me to be a genius at investing. It merely shows that long-range planning pays off much better than spur-of-the-moment moves. The same may be said of short-range planning.

Some Ground Rules

Regardless of where anyone stands in terms of financial life, whether buying the first savings bond or first share of stock, or contemplating revising a substantial financial program, one question should be asked: "What are my objectives?"

Not long ago I was asked by an elderly woman to go over her financial arrangements with her.

"What are you concerned about? What do you want to accomplish?"

She knew. She told me at once that she was concerned about financially safeguarding a daughter. Secondly, she was seeking a way to improve her income from investments. She knew her objectives.

Shortly after that I talked with a young career woman. She had reached the point at which she had some money "to do something with." She did not know what. We began talking about her objectives. What did she anticipate or plan for five or ten years down the road? Keeping in mind the flexibility needed at her age, we could then begin to discuss how best to meet her purposes.

Begin by deciding your purposes.

What Purposes?

For you, I do not know. That is something which each must decide on a purely personal basis, and that means with consideration for purely personal problems, choices, and outlook. Some common considerations are: relatives dependent upon you, children to be educated, economic hazards of disability in your own situation, likelihood of adequate pension, preferences and abilities as to handling money matters, even personal attitudes toward your own self-sufficiency. There are dozens of others.

Unless you are a person who can arrange thought processes well, and then remember the results of them, it will probably be worth your while to make a list of what you conceive to be your short and long-range objectives. After you have done that, put the list aside for a few days, then review it. Do not be surprised if you think you should make some changes. If you do, make them. Repeat the process two or three times if necessary.

Next, break down your list into short and long-range objectives. This will not only be of help to you in your own thinking, but it will be of great help to you later on. Eventually you will be discussing your financial and estate affairs with those who will be guiding you in various respects. Your lists will keep you on the track, and will enable you to clarify for your advisers what it is that you really want to accomplish.

Finally, be mindful that just because you have established your objectives, you are not necessarily set for life. To follow some of the same considerations indicated as being typical, think what may occur. The dependent relative may die. The children will finish high school and perhaps college. Disability and pension plans may be greatly improved by the company where you work, or possibly by the company where your husband works. You (especially after reading this book!) may find that your own attitudes and interests regarding the handling of money, investments, insurance, and other estate assets have changed.

In any event, a good rule is to review your objectives as well as your plans at least every two years, or upon the happening of a major change in your circumstances or responsibilities.

Information Please

The radio show of the thirties by that name consisted of a panel of experts who tried, usually successfully, to answer questions submitted by the listening audience, but presented "cold" to the panel.

That is a good game to play with yourself, but not with your attorney, insurance representative, trust officer, accountant, or financial adviser. Raise the questions about objectives, and what your present assets are. Then, to the extent possible get the information pertinent to the question. Many times you will find your own answer.

Many times I have inquired, "How is that stock held: jointly or individually?" or "Who is the beneficiary of that policy you just mentioned?" And many a time the answer has come back, "I don't know. I'll have to check."

Here is an example. One businesswoman, a competent one in her own enterprise, was working with me in assembling the final details we needed before going to her attorney to have her will prepared. In going over her life insurance policies I found one which would mature in about two years for $10,000. She was delighted. She had not realized it. Needless to say that changed the view on short-range plans.

It is possible to secure from an employer details and present status of an individual account under the company's pension or profit-sharing plan. Knowledge of what such a plan means to you or to your husband, now or in the future, is important to planning.

How important can be illustrated by the case of a young friend of mine. Recently he was offered a position with another company which was ready to hire him at once.

Fortunately, he knew the terms of his present company's pension plan. He told his employer-to-be that he could not make the change for 60 days. By staying in the old job that much longer he was able to vest, i.e. acquire a non-forfeitable right in, the pension plan of the company where he had worked for a number of years. Failure to have stayed for the additional time would have cost him thousands of dollars toward the fund which will ultimately provide him a pension from his old employer.

So, information please—all you can gather about your present holdings and circumstances. You "can't get there from here" without knowing where "here" is.

Professional Guidance

Size alone does not necessarily determine simplicity in the planning or conduct of financial affairs.

I think of one man who, with his brother, is trying to hold together a family business. It is a precarious situation. The man's financial worth is certainly not very substantial, but his financial affairs are not simple: money tied up in inventory and equipment, accounts receivable, mortgages on home and business building, and so on.

Contrast that to another situation in which the individual owns stock valued at about three million dollars. His objective and plans (whatever their merits may be) call for retaining all that stock which constitutes practically his entire estate. He does not want to sell, diversify, give, or otherwise alter total retention. His worth is obviously much greater than that of the man in the previous example, but his day-to-day concerns, planning, changing, and even his estate settlement could very easily be more readily accomplished than that of the man whose net worth is a small fraction of his.

The point in contrasting these two actual cases is that size does not automatically determine complexity. Neither does it, alone, dictate the extent of need for professional advice, craftsmanship, and draftsmanship in arranging and following through with a plan.

What advice? What counsel? What professionals?

The lawyer. Perhaps you already have an attorney whom you count as "my lawyer." If so, fine. In that event you may skip the rest of this section about lawyers.

If not, then you are like those of us who have moved from city to city over the years, and each time have had to find a suitable doctor. It is not the easiest task, but it needs doing.

You may be saying to yourself, "Yes, but I don't need a lawyer with the urgency I might need a physician."

No? It would be a bit awkward, would it not, to try to select an attorney following a midnight automobile accident for which you were being held?

Trust Officer. Much of the same as above can be said equally well in the case of a trust officer. Questions you may have in the future on many of the subjects covered in Chapters Seven, Eight, and Nine can be answered for you, in your particular circumstances, by a competent trust officer.

You may feel that you will never use trust services or become a trust customer. But again, you may. One never knows. In any case, the trust officer will be glad to talk with you.

Investment Adviser. When you need a specialist, go to a specialist. Cousin Charlie who just heard down at the plant where he works that Slurpy-Glurpy Sundae Sauce stock is a great buy, and will soon double in price, hardly qualifies as an investment expert.

Investment advisers range from individuals and firms who specialize in advisory services only, on a fee basis, to account executives in brokerage houses. The good ones are interested in strengthening the client's portfolio *in accordance with objectives*, not just in making sales.

A member of the National Association of Securities Dealers has not only passed rigorous examinations, but has also subscribed to the association's code of ethics.

The availability of services and competent personnel ranges widely, often in proportion to the size of the community. You may already have satisfactory counsel as to your investments. If not, your best bet is to make local inquiry of qualified people. Unless you live in a very small community you should be able to secure at least a couple of names.

Insurance Adviser: It is likely that being a reader of this book you already have an insurance person upon whom you depend. Perhaps you have two: one for life, one for property and casualty. Or, you may have one person who handles all forms. It does not matter as long as you receive good advice and service.

For at least forty years the argument has been going on as to whether having one agent for all lines has any real advantage over having one agent for life coverages, and another for property and casualty protection. The mere fact that the argument has not been settled either ideologically or competitively should be proof enough that it does not matter as long as the results in counsel and service to you are good.

The professional designations of C.L.U. (Chartered Life Underwriter) and C.P.C.U. (Chartered Property and Casualty Underwriter) are indications of persons who have passed rigorous examinations and who have subscribed to codes of ethics and conduct. There are many other fine insurance people who do not hold these designations, but who are extremely competent.

If you presently do not have satisfactory insurance guidance, and if you are at a loss as to where to turn, make inquiry locally—perhaps of some of the other advisers suggested above.

Other. There are other types of advisers who may be needed from time to time, or upon particular occasion. If you buy or sell real estate probably you will want to use the services of a real estate expert. If you need a jewelry appraisal for insurance or estate purposes you will need an expert. And so on.

Two other kinds of professional advisers should be mentioned: accountants (C.P.A.'s or others) and tax service people. There is some degree of overlap in that accountants may prepare individual tax returns, though many are not eager for that sort of work. (Some attorneys will prepare tax returns, but many will not.)

Many women prepare their own returns. I know the wife of one physician who does the joint return for herself and her husband—and a physician's return is not a simple one to complete.

There are matters other than tax work which definitely call for the use of an accountant's knowledge and skill. It pays to seek out such help when needed.

Some women like to work with figures, do not mind fighting the battle of forms, and like the satisfaction of doing as much tax and other "figure work" as they can. Others have neither the knowledge nor the interest in such. These should utilize the services of professionals.

This is true for men as well as for women. I have a friend, a retired executive, whose wife always took care of the tax work. Recently she died, so now my friend has turned to a professional.

If it costs a little to rid yourself of what for you would be a worrisome chore, so what?

Your Funds

It happens that as I am writing this chapter I am also engaged in preparing for a nearby college a seminar designed for women in small business. In connection with this, I have been looking over an exhibit prepared by the head of the Economics Department. In it there is a salient distinction made between *fixed* and *controllable* expenses. Any of us who have operated businesses are well aware of the difference. It is not only a true one in business, it is true in personal financial control as well.

The individual, too, has *fixed* expenses about which little, if anything, can be done: taxes, housing, food and clothing (within reason), transportation, etc. These are operating costs which require operating funds.

Next comes a group of *controllable* expenses: vacation (plush or Spartan), level of contributions, level of spending for furniture and furnishings, kind of new car chosen, etc.

This is a good point at which to talk briefly about budgets.

If you are one of those rare women who never prepared, followed, or even contemplated a budget, then now is the time to put aside this book for awhile. Talk with someone who can assist you in setting up a budget. This may be your insurance adviser, your banker, or a friend who has had some experience with budgets. There are pamphlets available, perhaps from your banker or insurance adviser. The best bet, however, is a face-to-face talk with a qualified person. If you have had no budgeting experience you will be surprised at the relief you will feel once you have a proper budget in operation.

I think of one intelligent woman who recently had been widowed. She had no trouble in setting up the expense side of her budget, but she was terribly concerned, almost overwhelmed, when she attempted to lay out the income side which her husband had always handled. Her income did not all come in monthly. A considerable portion of it came from A.T. & T. stock, the dividends of which are paid quarterly. For her this seemed to distort the whole income picture.

Once she saw a month-by-month spread on paper as to which months were her big income months, and how the totals put her in comfortable position, and how all she had to do was allocate from the big income months to the lower income months, she was almost a changed person. She was truly relieved.

If all of that seems simplistic, it is spelled out only because it leads to the vital purpose of this book.

After the *fixed* and *controllable* classifications there should come another form of outlay for most persons: savings and investment. Note, however, certain facts.

1. What remains for savings and investment is determined in large measure by what allocations have been made to *controllable* expenses.

2. The OBJECTIVES for what is to be allocated to the savings and investment accounts should be determined individually. Later needs for capital? For income? Adequacy of anticipated pension? Expected inheritance?

Few people can put aside the maximum desirable to obtain hoped-for objectives. Few readers, however, cannot make a start and improve on it as times goes on.

3. There are some people who do not need to be concerned about saving and investing. These include: persons of wealth, retirees who "have enough to see them through," and persons who are dependent upon others for reasons of age, disability, or whatever.

All of this deserves thought, and the thought should begin with determination of OBJECTIVES.

Change

This chapter began with a "must": *always start*

with objectives. It is fitting that it nears its close with another "must": *be alert to change; then take appropriate action.*

One career woman had named her parents as beneficiaries of a life insurance policy. It took me several years after they died to get her to take the *appropriate action* of changing the beneficiary. Why? I really do not know. I think it was because she did not like to think about anything having to do with death. Since that time she has died. Had the change not been effected, the money from the claim payment would have been paid to her estate, and so settled under the terms of her will. This would have meant that the persons who were eventually named as beneficiaries would not have been the recipients. Change!

One couple worked. Each had a good job. At home they tolerated each other for years. Finally, they divorced. The wife had just as much income from her job as before, but what a difference in the whole range of her expenses. Change!

Very likely you can think of a dozen examples of different changes among people you know. Income goes up or down. Health changes. Dependents die; others become dependent. Occasionally windfalls occur. Sometimes losses jolt. Change!

Change is certain. When it does come it calls for *appropriate action* as soon as possible. Financial success demands *being alert to change* so that *appropriate action* can be taken.

Overstreet wrote that the mark of the mature mind is resilience. So, too, is it the mark of maturity in the conduct of financial affairs.

Questions on Chapter One

1. What is the extremely important first step in approaching financial and estate planning?

2. What two kinds of objectives are there, and what is necessary in determining them?

3. What is the maximum time you should allow between reviews of your plans?

4. What are the best ways to look for professional guidance if you have none?

5. What two kinds of expenses are there, and why is it necessary to distinguish between them?

6. Change calls for what?

II

Spending and Saving
... What and How

Changes to look for—Spending: fixed and controllable expenses—Rules for checking accounts—Savings: differences between saving and investing—How much savings—Rules for savings accounts—Savings institutions—NOW accounts.

More Change

The last chapter closed on a note of change. That provides a good transition to this chapter which begins with the same subject, change.

Spending and saving involve the individual with banking, and banking is undergoing tremendous change. Within the next fifteen years there probably will be as many significant changes in banking as in any other business, and almost certainly more change than in any similar period of banking history.

To be aware of what is changing now, and what will be changing in the years immediately ahead is to be free of surprise, misunderstanding, and disturbance when the changes affect you.

The electronic age, especially through computerized adaptations, is revolutionizing traditional banking practices and services. How soon you will see these changes in your bank depands upon a number of factors, such as: size of your bank, type of customer it serves, location, individual bank policy, what it deems its market to be, what its competitive situation is, whether it is locally owned and managed or part of a larger organization, and how its officials and its board of directors evaluate costs of changes vs. advantages and efficiencies thereof.

Some of these changes are already here. All are technically possible. Some will come more quickly and be more widespread than others.

We have already seen the advent of the "minibank," or the "24 hour bank," the unattended device through which with your properly coded entry you can make a deposit or a withdrawal.

Patterned along the same line, but more intricate, is the "automatic teller" which is designed to handle routine, over-the-counter transactions in the bank.

Direct deposits to individual accounts are now available for Social Security benefits, and some employers are utilizing direct deposits to employee accounts for payroll purposes. Look for an expansion of this worthwhile type of service to include dividend and interest payments and other regularly stipulated payments. No one can steal or forge a check made out to you when there is no check but only a direct deposit to your account.

Point-of-sale debits and credits will be here one of these days. The sales person or check-out person will enter your code and the amount of your purchase in the console or register. The response of approval or disapproval will be returned at once. If approved a charge will be made to your account in the bank and a corresponding credit will be made to the store's account.

Another change affects check clearances. Banks are already utilizing electronic data processing for inter-bank clearings. This means that checks clear more rapidly.

These are some of the changes which you are seeing, or will see as time goes on. They should provide convenience, security, and more efficient service for you. Be alert to them and to others.

The basic planning, rules, and handling of your personal finances will not change as a result of electronic wizardry. They may be affected by other causes, but not by that.

Spending

In the last chapter the distinction between *fixed* and *controllable* expenses was made. Now let us put them together for purposes of arriving at something else.

Taxes, housing, food, and other necessities are "musts." Add to them the *controllable* expenses you have decided upon. Deduct that total from total income, and what remains is what you have to save or invest. (Naturally, gifts or inheritances would be in addition to this result, but one can scarcely budget for gifts or inheritances.)

Incidentally, some *controllables* eventually become *fixed*. While you are deciding whether to buy a car which will cost you $200 a month to finance or one which will cost you $350 a month you are debating a *controllable* item. Once you make the choice you have added a *fixed* item to your monthly list of expenditures.

There is a point to be made here. It may be well illustrated by an experience I had not too long ago.

My wife and I were traveling in Africa. We had to change planes in one of the small emerging countries, which, in the interests of international relations, we shall allow to remain nameless.

After boarding the plane for our outgoing flight, I picked up a copy of what I imagine was the only newspaper in the country. The lead story concerned a recent meeting of businessmen of that country. They had been addressed by the president, and according to the article, he had said something like this to them. "You must remember that after you sell your goods you must not spend all of that money, or consider that to be your income. If you do not take some of it to buy new goods to replace the ones you have already sold you will soon be out of business. What you take in is not all profit.''

I could scarcely believe what I had read, but a re-reading convinced me. The purpose of relating this story is not to afford an excuse to comment on the level of economic knowledge of the audience in that country. Nor is it to imply the need of such caution to any reader who may be contemplating going into business.

It does provide an extreme example, however, in the matter of personal finance. We, too, dare not spend "all of that money," or we, too, shall someday be "out of business." Maintenance, replacements, and emergencies will come along sometime, so some preparation must be made for them.

This brings us back to budgeting (See Chapter One), and to the need for special funds to take care of these contingencies. Even that is not the core of our purpose now.

The real thrust of the story here is that these non-immediate requirements will have to be met someday. That being the case, the funds they will take cannot be a part of permanent savings or investment. More of that when we talk about savings. For now, don't spend "all of that money."

In today's economy, spending, except on the most basic level, involves the use of a checking account. A few rules which are applicable, whether you are a relatively new user of checking services or an old timer at it, will probably serve better than a long, detailed description of the subject.

Rule 1. Be sure that you have the kind of account best suited to your needs. Normally, a bank offers several types of accounts. One type may require maintenance of a minimum balance for a no-charge account. Another may offer no-charge checking if a savings account, perhaps with a specified minimum, is also maintained. Still another type will make a charge per check but no requirement of minimum balance. Some banks may simply make no charge and may even offer an inducement to boot. There can be other variations, too, which are sometimes complicated.

If you are not certain that you have the best type of account for your purposes, discuss the subject with your banker. What is best for you may change. The kind of account which best suited you when you first started to work, and had a few dollars left from your weekly check, may not be best suited to you now that you are a well-established career woman or a household accounts manager. If you are not sure, talk with your banker.

Rule 2. Do not keep too much money in a checking account. To this you may be saying, "Who does?" To which I would reply, "You might be surprised."

I recall sitting with a professional man and his wife in the initial planning interview, ascertaining their assets. I learned that they kept a balance of about $20,000 in a checking account.

"Why that much in a checking account?"

"Well, we might need it sometime—maybe in the business and in a hurry."

"Has that ever happened?"

"No."

"Is it very likely to happen?"

"Probably not."

"Is it conceivable that you really are not likely to need more than perhaps a third of that amount for some sort of emergency?"

Pause. "Well, yes, that should be enough."

As a result they reduced the balance to about $7,000 and put the remainder to work at a good rate of interest.

Your working balance may not need to be $7,000; it may be a few hundred. Too much for one person is not necessarily too much for another.

Give *Rule 2* a thought.

Rule 3. Do not keep too little in a checking account. You may make just a small error in your checkbook arithmetic and overdraw your account because you were running too close to the line, and that would probably cost you a few dollars in overdraft charge. Then, too, you might need to write a check in an emergency for an amount in excess of your too-small balance. Furthermore, if ever you give your bank as a credit reference your banker will not be able to say that you keep a normal balance in your account, let alone a substantial balance.

Rule 4. Be wary of putting the account in joint names with anyone other than your spouse. This rule is even more important as it applies to savings accounts so it will be covered under that subject later in the chapter.

Some Other Aspects of Spending

No "bargain" is a bargain if you do not need or really want the product or service. I once knew a woman who bought for a very cheap price several cartons of canned vegetables, all in good condition, no spoilage. The reason for the bargain was that water in the grocer's basement had soaked off all the labels. I never did understand what sort of bargain that was for her—not knowing as she opened a can while preparing dinner if she would have lima beans or red beets.

That may be extreme, but one does not "save" (as the commercials say) by acquiring a product one would not otherwise buy. In money matters, there are situations in which you can almost create your own bargains. If you have a bill which allows a discount if paid early, there is a bargain. Use it. You can bet that business people try to take the discounts offered on bills they receive.

If you have an unneeded $500 earning five percent in a savings account, or no interest in a checking account, and you also have a balance due on a note or on an installment account for which you are paying a much higher rate of interest, pay it off if the terms permit you to do so and save the interest. There is your bargain.

Look for discounts, deductions, and prepayment possibilities to reduce spending. The range may be anywhere from pennies to many dollars.

Saving

At this point some distinctions between saving and investing should be made.

Savings will likely be in cash or its equivalent such as U.S. Savings Bonds. Investments will put the cash to work in real estate, securities, perhaps a business venture, and so on.

Savings will likely have a fixed or relatively stable rate of return. An investment may, or may not, but it will likely hold hope or guarantee of a larger return than savings.

Savings will likely be in smaller amounts than investments. You can save dimes or quarters; you cannot very well invest them until you have a large amount of them. Investments will normally be in larger amounts than savings.

Savings are more likely to be for shorter durations and/or immediate withdrawals than investments. You save for vacation funds, for some special project some months or a year away, or perhaps for a downpayment on a new car. You would be more likely to invest for retirement, for college purposes if some years off, or to enhance your total assets for long-range purposes.

With that by way of background, let us move on to some specifics about savings.

How Much Saving

A couple of weeks ago I read that one woman who is an expert in finance stated that there "usually should be the equal of two months' income" in savings. About forty years ago one of the standard texts on investments stated that there should be "at least an amount equal to two or three months' income" in a savings account. Forty years should validate the idea.

Certainly the reason is obvious: to provide quick cash for an emergency of whatever nature.

—and what else?

In addition to this basic amount which is primarily an emergency fund, there will be other specific purposes for which you will want to save: a vacation some months hence, a new car, a down payment on a house or lot, college educations if they are near-term (if long-term you may want to invest until closer to the time), and so on.

Generally, specific purpose funds should not be invested, because you want to be sure that your funds plus a reasonable return will be available when you are ready for that vacation or that new car. Should you invest the money and then find that when you wanted it the stock market had become depressed, or the business venture was really pushed for cash, you might not be able to retrieve even the amount you had invested, let alone have a profit.

There is another specific purpose fund and that is an accumulation fund for investing. It is designed to build up a sufficient amount to warrant investing, probably for long-range ends: larger retirement fund, fund from which the income and possibly gains will enhance your current income, fund for whatever purposes you might wish, be they plans to go into business for yourself, or whatever.

Rules for Saving

The rules for savings are much the same as those given for checking accounts.

Rule 1. Be sure that you have the best kind of account for you. In the case of savings: at least your basic savings account, which means privilege of immediate withdrawal, best available interest rate (more on this below), and reasonable accessibility. (There would be no point in driving five miles across town to get ¼ percent more interest on a $500 account.) Competition tends to keep interest rates paid by various institutions reasonably close, but there *are* exceptions. So look around.

Rule 2. Don't keep too much in a savings account. I once knew of two sisters who maintained a $30,000 ordinary savings account. They could have invested most of it at a considerably higher rate of return.

Rule 3. Don't keep too little in savings. In the first place, a too-small amount will not meet the test of "equivalent to two months' income." In the second place, a very small amount scarcely justifies the bother of maintaining both a savings and a checking account.

Rule 4. Be sure you know exactly what you are doing if you decide to open a joint account.

Many people think that by so doing they will avoid taxes at death especially in the cases of husband and wife. Not necessarily so.

State laws vary. One state levies an inheritance tax (one-third if three joint holders, etc.) when one of the joint holders dies. When I pointed this out to one man who had a joint account with "mother-in-law to take care of her out of her own funds" he quickly changed it.

Another state does the same but allows for adjustment if it can be proved that the surviving joint holder actually contributed a portion.

States with community property laws have different provisions.

The Federal Estate Tax applies to the entire amount of the joint account in the estate of the first to die unless it can be proved that the survivor contributed a certain amount. If that can be proved, and it is not always easy to do it, then the tax is levied accordingly. (See, also, Chapter Nine.)

One out of every so many joint accounts comes to grief in other ways. An absconding husband or wife who withdraws almost all of the funds in a joint account, and then takes off for far places would not be the first to do so. This is certainly not counsel never to have a joint account. Most joint accounts, especially the household accounts of husband and wife work out quite satisfactorily. There is, however, a great amount of misinformation on the subject of joint accounts bandied about. All of this leads to the caveat: *Be sure that you understand what the ramifications of a joint account are before you commit yourself to one. Your banker or your attorney can counsel you.*

Savings Institutions

Banks, mutual savings banks (in some states), and savings and loan companies all offer savings services of various kinds.

Most insure their accounts up to various state and/or federal limits, explanations of which are readily available.

Maximum interest rates and certain other restrictions are dictated by state and/or federal laws and regulations. There will be some differences in interest rates paid for similar accounts nonetheless. One small difference may be only that of whether the interest is compounded daily, quarterly or semi-annually. Presently there is also a difference in that savings and loan institutions and mutual savings banks are allowed to pay a ¼ percent higher maximum interest rate than are commercial banks.

Passbook accounts of the "withdraw anytime" sort do not pay as much as do other accounts which require advance notification of withdrawal, or which are made for a definite duration of the deposit.

Certificates of deposit, which are often referred to as "C.D's," and savings certificates which have durations of several months or years will pay higher returns, but there are penalties for early withdrawals. Interest return will vary with the state of the money market at the time of purchase and with the duration of the certificate. It is important to understand the terms, especially as to permissability of early withdrawal, penalties therefor, and rate of return.

The sisters with the $30,000 mentioned previously might well have put a large part of that money into some sort of certificate. They would have earned considerably more interest with safety. Even in the unlikely event that they would have had to withdraw the money before the maturity date, they would have lost only a few months' interest, a small risk to take as opposed to the higher return they might have had. True—their interest would have been reduced to the passbook rate—but their only hazard under the rules at the time was that of losing three months' interest at the lower rate they would have received, had they not bought a certificate.

Another channel for savings is a credit union. If you belong to one you might investigate what arrangements it offers to members.

Once the sound, basic savings account has been established for immediate or emergency needs, the use of certificates for further savings should be considered.

NOW

The last chapter closed with the subject of change. This chapter began with the same subject. It will close with a current and important example.

The nature of it is such that it could have been placed in the treatment of checking accounts, or, since it is a hybrid, it could have been a part of the section on savings.

The name of this form of account is NOW. The acronym stands for Negotiable Order of Withdrawal. A NOW account combines the advantages of a checking account with the interest bearing advantages of a savings account. From the user's standpoint, the negotiable order of withdrawal performs the functions of a check.

I have before me an announcement of NOW services being offered by a large New England bank. It states that 5% daily compounded interest will be paid on NOW accounts. If a minimum balance of $300 is maintained there is no service charge.

NOW accounts are not available everywhere at this time. Terms may vary from bank to bank where the accounts are available. Their convenience and advantages are obvious, so it would be well to remain on the lookout for their introduction in your community.

Undoubtedly there will be changes and refinements in them as times goes on, but it appears that in many instances they will serve satisfactorily in one account what it has heretofore taken two accounts to do.

Congress is engaged in a study pointed toward major changes in permissible bank practices regarding the whole subject of checking, savings, and interest. Watch for changes.

Change is NOW; NOW is change.

Questions on Chapter Two

1. What are some of the changes happening and soon to happen in banking, and what do they mean to you?

2. Why is it important to distinguish between *fixed* and *controllable* expenses?

3. What rules of good practice apply to checking accounts?

4. How are savings distinguished from investments?

5. What should determine the amount of savings for you?

6. What rules of good practice apply to savings accounts?

7. What is NOW, and why might NOW be important to you?

III

Insurance

Insuring properly—Basic rules—Reasons for
life insurance—Common types—Annuities—
Accident and sickness, disability insurance—
Hospitalization, Blue Cross and Blue Shield
coverages—"General lines"—Property and
casualty insurance—Final considerations.

Insuring Properly

After establishment of the basic savings account
described in the previous chapter, the next step in a
sound financial program is that of acquiring an
adequate amount of life insurance. So says the textbook of forty years ago mentioned before. So says an
advertisement of one of the largest brokerage firms.
So would say most of the people engaged in financial
planning whom I have known. I cannot recall a single
one whom I have ever heard voice disagreement.

For that reason insurance will be the subject of this
chapter rather than investments which one might

think of as the next most logical consideration. This is also a good place to include other forms of coverage including property and casualty coverages. Insurance of various forms begins to assume importance at this stage of personal financial development.

Why is it such an important consideration in creating, conserving, and disposing of an estate?

A single bad automobile accident for which you are liable can wipe away years of savings and investment if you are not properly insured.

One fire can consume years of frugal efforts as well as your property if you are not properly insured.

Disability can terminate necessary income if you are not adequately insured.

Most importantly, premature death can spoil your estate plans, prevent completion of the objectives you want to accomplish, and terminate your efforts to provide for loved ones. It can cancel your hopes of being able to make gifts to favorite charities or persons, and it can leave your estate short of ready cash for last expenses and taxes. Again, insurance can hedge those risks.

Two Rules and Some Examples

The first basic rule for insurance is this: *Whenever possible insure against losses which you reasonably*

*cannot absorb yourself; in general, do not insure
against losses which you reasonably can absorb.*

Here is one example of the operation of the rule.
One summer during my younger daughter's college
career she found herself a job which would take her
to the opposite end of the city from where we lived.
She needed a car good enough to get her back and
forth. I bought an old one for her, one which I had
no intention of keeping after she returned to college.
It ran, but it certainly was not worth much.

Nevertheless, she could have an accident for which
she might be held liable. Risk that I reasonably could
not assume: liability; risk that I could afford to carry
on such an old car: collision. I insured accordingly.
(More will be said about these coverages later in the
chapter.)

This rule is important enough to warrant another
example. A young friend was leaving one employer
to work for another. Under the insurance plans for
employees of the new employer there was a waiting
period before the insurance of a new employee
became effective.

Hospitalization, surgery, and death are fairly
sizable risks to assume on one's own. I advised him
to buy coverage for the interim period, and then
decide after the waiting period, and after acquainting
himself with the provisions of the new coverage how
much, if any, of the coverage bought for the interim
he would retain. This was another case of hedging
a risk which was not a reasonable one for self-
insurance.

These examples lead to our second rule: *Review your needs and your insurance at least every two years or upon any major change in your economic or family situation.*

The reason for the rule is that the risks you can afford to carry within reason change with the passing of time—either way. You may find that the proper amount of coverage for you is greater or less than it had been.

Now let us combine the rules in another example. Near where I camped as a boy there lived an old fellow—well, he seemed old to me then—who was a real hermit. He had a little shack in the woods where he lived midst huckleberries, copperheads, and stands of beautiful old trees. When he needed money to buy a few staples Huck would go to one of the farms a couple of miles away and hire himself out for long enough to earn some money for his groceries.

It is inconceivable that Huck ever thought about insurance. If his shack were to burn, or blow down in a storm, all he had to do would be cut timber and rebuild. What need for any insurance there?

He had no known family or relatives, and was responsible to or for no one but himself. Had he become disabled, or when he died it simply would have been up to the state or county to take care of the expenses. In short, there were no risks he could not absorb either by a little work in erecting a new shack, or by working for a few dollars to replace whatever he might lose.

Now, suppose that through some freak of circumstance you had come into possession of Huck's little shack. As long as you kept it merely as a shelter and loafing place for an outing in the woods, you, too, would most likely not have considered insurance seriously, if at all. After all, what risk was there that you could not readily absorb?

But later on had you decided to "do something with it," and make a real weekend retreat, or possibly a summer home out of it, then you would have wanted to do something about insuring the place. You would have passed the bounds of that part of *Rule One* having to do with not insuring the risk you can afford to carry. You would have been encountering *Rule Two* which calls for reconsideration when a major change occurs. You would no longer have wanted to assume a risk then of several thousand dollars. Furthermore, as you continued to make improvements you would have found periodic reviews becoming important.

These same rules apply to life insurance as well as to other forms.

Life Insurance

Why do women buy life insurance? A simplistic answer would be, "for the same reason men do." A more complete answer could involve a lengthy dissertation on the subject. Perhaps some examples of actual cases will afford the best answer.

1. *It costs money to die.* One day I received a telephone call. "This is Helen," said the voice at the other end of the line. "I must see you—and soon."

"Well," I replied, "that's always a pleasure, but what's up?"

"My mother died a couple of weeks ago, and I just have found out what it costs to die. I want you to tell me what I should do about my life insurance. I know I don't have enough."

She had just realized that she had crossed the line between a risk which she reasonably could assume and one she ought not assume.

2. *It takes money to complete financial or estate plans.* The sister of one of my good friends had just lost her husband. She had been left with two children barely in their teens. She had decided to buy a small house for their home. She wanted to be sure that if she were to die the home would be free and clear for the children. (That would not have been my goal, but it was hers, and she was firm in her objective. Remember "Objectives" from Chapter One?) The answer to completing that objective was the acquisition of life insurance in an amount sufficient to pay off the mortgage if she should die before she had cleared it.

3. *It takes money to care for dependents (not necessarily children).* A friend of mine, a very able executive, had two members left in her immediate family: a brother in a mental institution and an aged mother who was failing mentally and physically. The

brother had a veteran's disability pension, and would be taken care of for life.

The mother, who was in a nursing home, was of great concern to my friend. There was enough income and capital to see the mother through if all went as at present, but if rates increased much more, or if major medical expenses had to be incurred, then what?

My friend could handle even increased costs as long as she was living and working. But if she were to pre-decease her mother? That was the question. What other answer was there but life insurance?

Speaking of dependents: husbands are dependents in a real economic sense, whether or not the wife is employed. Think of the economic consequences to a household when a wife dies. That is one reason that there are millions of dollars of life insurance on the lives of housewives.

Many households today literally are dependent upon two incomes. If the standard of living is to be maintained, and that standard has been dependent upon two incomes to support it, what happens if death eliminates one of those incomes? Indeed, it is not unusual for the wife's income to be the larger. Why then is it not essential that indemnification be provided against the loss of her income just as well as that of her husband?

More than one study has been made of the dollar value of all the household and family care services of the wife who is not engaged in outside employment.

The studies do not agree as to any exact figure, but they do agree that the value of those services is several thousand dollars a year.

Insurance should be seriously considered for wives, whether or not they are employed outside the home.

4. *It takes money to pay inheritance and estate taxes.* Neither Uncle Sam nor your state is amenable to accepting a car, or a house, or jewelry in payment of taxes. Only dollars will do. I think of one woman, 57, of another, 35, and of another, 60, all of whom acquired life insurance to be sure that death taxes could be met without disturbing other estate assets.

5. *It takes money to pay off loans.* One woman had used the fund she had put aside for college educations for children, but there still remained a couple of years of tuition ahead. A loan from a friend was negotiated. The lender was not fearful of repayment as long as the borrower lived, but he wanted assurance of repayment otherwise. Life insurance collateralized the loan, and hedged the possibility of death.

6. *It takes money to "square up" various business arrangements at death.* According to recent government figures there are nearly 500,000 women conducting their own businesses as sole proprietors, partners, or stockholders.

One woman owns a business in conjunction with two brothers. One of the brothers works in the business; the other does not. If their sister dies the brothers do not want her stock sold to anyone outside the family. Through a formal agreement and the use of life insurance on her life their objective has been assured.

These are only some of the reasons why women buy life insurance. We have not even touched on reasons of retirement, the place of annuities, the accumulation of special purpose funds, and numerous others.

Purpose of Life Insurance

The late Dr. S. S. Huebner of the University of Pennsylvania's Wharton School of Business, and the man who had the original concept for establishing The American College of Life Underwriters (now The American College), gave as the primary function of life insurance, "the indemnification against the economic loss of the human life value."

If you will look back at the reasons given above as to why many women have felt the need of life insurance you will see that the function of the insurance in most instances has been just that.

Common Types of Life Insurance

(These explanations are not meant to be technically precise or detailed. They are designed for ease of understanding by one not familiar with the language or terms of insurance.)

Term: a type of insurance issued for a particular period of time, e.g. a year, two years, ten years, perhaps to age 65. It may or may not be renewable at the end of its term.

Except in the long-term contracts it usually builds no cash values.

Premiums are low at younger ages, but if policy is renewable rates will increase upon renewal.

In general it is designed to afford protection for temporary needs, whether the temporary period be a couple of years or many years, as in the case of term insurance covering the unpaid balance of a mortgage.

Ordinary Life: insurance which calls for coverage and premium payments during life. Depending upon the mortality table used it will mature to the policy owner at a very advanced age of the insured, such as 100.

Premium is constant in amount. Cash values are built. If premiums are discontinued, cash surrender value may be taken, or insurance may be extended for some period, or paid-up insurance for a reduced amount may be elected.

Limited Payment Life: Same as above except through payment of higher premiums the premium paying period is reduced to a specific number of years. Twenty-Payment Life, and Life Paid-Up at 65 are examples.

 Endowment, Retirement Income, Income Endowment: These policies mature at specified times for specified sums, or for incomes produced by those sums, or at prior death. Examples: 20-Year Endowment (matures for face amount at end of 20 years or prior death). Retirement Income at 65 (matures for so much specified sum, or for specified monthly income for life thereafter, or at death prior to 65 pays a specified sum).

There are numerous other policy forms and combinations and variations of the above.

It has been said above that cash values are built under the terms of certain policies. This is true in what insurance people call "permanent" policies as opposed to term policies. One advantage of the cash value feature is that although an interest factor is applied to the cash value that interest is not subject to income tax on a year-by-year basis. Neither is it taxed as income at death of the insured. If the policy is surrendered in later years when the cash value has exceeded net premiums paid then the gain is taxed as ordinary income. At that time, however, the insured may be in a lower tax bracket than in earlier years.

Meanwhile for that investment portion the policy owner has had professional management (the insurance company's investment department), and a continually totally invested fund (the cash value), something not easy to achieve in personally invested funds.

There are those who argue that term insurance should be bought and the difference invested. When comparisons are made the theory is usually supported by assumptions of all funds being totally and continuously invested, of little or no purchase costs for investments, and of a moderately high and steady rate of return, and, of course, of self-discipline in always investing the difference.

Experts may be able to meet all of those requirements. Few people that I have known do.

There is one other very real consideration which I have seen rise to haunt one who depended upon term for a total insurance program. Most companies will not continue term coverage beyond some certain age, and term premiums become quite high in those later years of life, the very times one usually wants decreased, not increased outlays.

Your insurance adviser can show you comparisons between term and "permanent" forms. Each has its place. The trick is to keep each in its proper place.

Something about Annuities

Annuities are usually bought from life insurance companies, so this is perhaps as good a place as any to say something about them.

They have been called, "the upside down principle of life insurance, life insurance providing the orderly creation of an estate, and annuities providing the orderly distribution of an estate.''

An annuity pays an amount, usually monthly, to the recipient who is called ''the annuitant.'' Normally an annuity pays for the lifetime of the annuitant, but it may have other guarantees, or it may be ''temporary.''

A *temporary annuity* pays for only a specified (temporary) period, not for life.

A *life annuity* pays the annuitant for the remainder of her or his lifetime—period.

A *refund annuity* does the same but additionally guarantees to pay enough money to someone, the annuitant or a beneficiary, to equal the original purchase price of the annuity. If the annuitant dies before receiving an equivalent of the original amount in payments, then the balance will be paid to the beneficiary either in continuing installment payments (installment refund annuity), or in a lump sum payment (cash refund annuity).

An *installment certain annuity* pays to the annuitant for life but also guarantees that payments will continue to someone, annuitant or beneficiary, until payments for a certain period such as 10 or 20 years in all have been made.

A *joint annuity* is payable on the basis of more than one life. There are numerous variations in terms.

The *variable annuity* is a relatively recent development. It does not guarantee a fixed amount of income because the annuity funds are totally or partially invested in equities, usually stock. The theory is that the annuitant will participate in the general growth of the economy, will have a hedge against inflation, and over a long period will profit by improved earnings of the invested funds as well as by capital gains.

Conversely, of course, the value of the fund may go down; there may be capital losses rather than gains; the annuity payments may be lower rather than higher.

Here is an actual case history of one such fund into which no new money was placed, and from which no withdrawals were made during the period shown.

Year end 1971		$12,733
,, ,, 1972		14,906
,, ,, 1973		12,201
,, ,, 1974		8,424
,, ,, 1975		11,125
,, ,, 1976		13,483

A thorough understanding of what the variable annuity is and how it works, as well as its advantages and disadvantages is essential before making a commitment. As the above shows, its value, and hence its return may go up or down.

A *deferred annuity* is one under the terms of which the starting date for the income is deferred to a date sometime in the future.

A *retirement annuity* is essentially a form of deferred annuity. The annuity fund is accumulated over a period of years through premium deposits. The starting date for payments to the annuitant customarily is sometime around retirement age, hence the name.

Life Insurance and You

Do you need some life insurance? Or more life insurance? If so, how much? What kind? What about an annuity?

First of all, start with objectives. Will life insurance help you achieve or assure them? Will owning some, or some more ease your mind? More than once I have heard people say after the acquisition of life insurance, "I'm glad that's done. I feel better now."

Next, having re-appraised the question in light of your objectives, be completely honest with yourself as to whether or not life insurance is the solution.

Not long ago I was conducting a seminar in estate planning for women. One participant held forth that she saw no need for life insurance. She had two children to put through college, so she had been buying government securities, and they were earning good interest, and so what was wrong with that?

I said, "Nothing as long as you live and keep up

your purchases, but where will the college money come from if you do not live?''

There was silence. She just looked at me and never did answer. I do not know to this day if the seriousness of the question had not occurred to her before, or if she knew that she was just ''running for luck'' and did not want to be reminded of it.

Finally, come as close as you can to what you think is a good answer to ''how much.'' There is an old rule of thumb for a breadwinner—and that is all it is, a rule of thumb—that life insurance should be no less than five times earned income. It is a general rule, certainly not applicable in all cases, some of which may call for more, some for less. For those who are not breadwinners for others than themselves there is no rule. It is just back to objectives!

After taking the above steps, then it is time to talk with your insurance adviser to help with the ''how much,'' and to let him or her guide you as to the proper type of policy best suited for you and your desired ends. The same steps apply to considerations of annuities.

* * * * * *

As in the case of life insurance, explanations of insurance coverages discussed in the remaining section of this chapter are not meant to be technically precise or complete as to all details. They are designed for general, basic understanding by those unfamiliar with insurance forms and language.

* * * * * *

Group Insurance

Insurance of different types often is made available to persons with a common employer, or who have a common affiliation as members of some association. Such insurance is group insurance. Its usual characteristics include:

No selection of risk by the insurer, i.e., if you qualify by virtue of employment or membership you are eligible. There will be certain requirements, however, such as length of service, need to make application within a certain time, etc.

Likelihood of lower premium than that available for individual purchases.

Specified schedule or limits as to coverage provided.

In the case of an employee, probability of payment of premiums by the employer.

Termination of coverage, or some sort of conversion to personal insurance upon cessation of employment or membership in the group.

If you are an employee you may be given any of several group coverages such as life, hospitalization, disability, or major medical. In other cases it will pay you to get full information, and then decide how the available insurance fits into your objectives and plans.

Accident and Sickness, Disability Insurance

The economic worth of the human life value can be eroded or lost by accident, or by conditions of health as well as by loss of life.

The loss may be of short duration or permanent. Whatever the reason, the loss of EARNED income is a serious matter. It means economic loss. If your income is unearned it normally is not affected by accident, sickness, or disability.

A wide choice of policies to insure against these hazards is available. There are different definitions of terms, durations for which benefits are payable, termination dates, provisions regarding cancellation, and premiums.

No more than a few thoughts on this vast subject can be offered here, but some questions to ask yourself are these.

Would loss of earned income jeopardize me financially?

How long could I afford to be without a paycheck following an accident or after the onset of disability resulting from off-the-job causes? (For on-the-job

occurrences inquire about your state's Workman's
Compensation Law.)

How long would my employer continue to pay me
at full scale? How long at a reduced figure? What is
his or her plan or policy?

Depending upon my answers to the above, how
long a waiting period (time after the accident or onset
of illness before any benefit is payable) should I consider if I buy coverage? Note: the longer the waiting
period the lower the premium.

Do I have enough facts at hand about this subject
to discuss it intelligently with my insurance adviser?

There is provision under Social Security laws for
disability income. Eligibility depends upon having an
adequate number of "covered quarters." Waiting
period is a minimum of five months. Requirements
to qualify are fairly and properly rigid.

Insurance for Hospitalization.
Blue Cross and Blue Shield

A common form of hospitalization insurance is a
flat amount of benefit for each day spent in a
hospital. It may include some other benefits, such as
provision through a surgical rider calling for certain
fixed amounts of benefits for different surgical
procedures.

Normally these policies are "fixed benefit" by

dollar amount per day for hospital stay and for surgery if that provision is included.

Blue Cross and Blue Shield benefits are on the basis of services rendered rather than on the basis of fixed dollar amounts.

The difference is this. Suppose that you and I have identical hospitalization policies which pay $30 per day for hospital confinement. You go to a hospital in your town which charges $80 per day, and I go to one in my city which charges $100 per day. Each of us will receive the same amount under our respective policies, $30 per day.

In the case of Blue Cross the benefit would be based upon the room charge, probably at semi-private rate. Surgical and other benefits are handled on the same "service rendered" basis limited by what is considered a "reasonable charge" in the particular community.

Private companies and Blue Cross/Blue Shield issue special coverages to supplement Medicare for charges which Medicare does not cover.

In this age of ever-increasing hospitalization and medical costs it is the part of wisdom to appraise one's own situation and then consider proper means of protection.

Information about their plans is readily available at Blue Cross and Blue Shield offices. Your insurance adviser can supply you with information about coverages marketed by commercial companies.

Medicare

Medicare benefits are provided through Social Security. Complete details can be secured through the nearest Social Security office. It is especially important for anyone approaching retirement age to find out about eligibility for, and provisions of Medicare.

There are a number of brochures on the subject which supply answers to most questions. The law, rules, and regulations are somewhat complex, so it is better not to rely on casually gathered information.

Major Medical and Catastrophe Insurance

The astronomical charges for service in connection with certain type of accidents, diseases, or conditions of health are frightening to contemplate.

There are policies available to insure against such high economic losses. Usually written with a "deductible," i.e., an amount for which you are responsible either on your own or through other insurance, they indemnify against the financial impact of large medical bills. Once your charges exceed the deductible then your major medical, or your catastrophe coverage steps in with its insurance. The larger the deductible amount the less the premium is.

These policies deserve consideration as a part of one's total financial planning.

Property, Casualty, and Liability Insurance

Property, casualty, and liability coverages are frequently referred to as "general lines." Included are: automobile, fire, homeowners, marine, hail, business interruption, and various forms of liability. There are numerous others as well.

Having lived in several states, I have observed, though I cannot prove, that there is much greater disparity among the states in regard to what property and casualty coverages are permitted than is the case with life insurance.

As an example, in the state where I previously lived I had a policy which I consider to be very worthwhile. I still should like to own it, but for some reason the Insurance Department of my present state does not allow the very same major company to issue it here.

All of this is by way of saying that these important general coverages require personal knowledge or good counsel. Perhaps the most helpful approach here is to point out some hazards and indicate the kinds of protection designed to indemnify against losses resulting from those hazards. The list is by no means complete. Other coverages may be secured by endorsements or different policies.

About the house:

Insurance

Fire or lightning;
Loss of personal prop-
erty general cov-
erage, scheduled
personal property
such as silverware,
jewelry;
Personal liability
(legal obligation to
pay damages);
Medical payments to
others resulting
from accident.

Combination coverages
such as in a Home-
owners policy, or
perhaps separate
policies in some
circumstances.

As to the automobile:

Bodily injury to others
for which you are
liable;
Property damage for
which you are
liable;
Medical payments
resulting from acci-
dent;
Collision (loss to the
automobile in excess
of the deductible
amount);
Bodily injury
sustained as a result
of accident with
uninsured motorist.

Usually, all or some
combination of cov-
erages contained in a
Family Automobile
policy.

These coverages should be reviewed at least every other year, or upon any major change such as the purchase of a new car, or the building of an addition of some sort to the house. For instance, you might not even buy collision insurance for a seven or eight-year-old car, but you certainly would want it if you bought a new one.

There are numerous other property and casualty forms of insurance available, as was indicated above. If the occasion arises to make you think of a hazard against which you wish to consider insuring, ask about it. There is a good possibility that your adviser can locate the proper coverage for you.

No doubt you have read some of the pros and cons of "no fault" insurance, a still relatively new form of coverage. As this is written, "no fault" is far from being nationwide in acceptance, and is by no means uniform in its provisions among those states which have adopted it. Watch for change of its status where you live.

Some Final Considerations

1. Give thought to the relationship of the amount of premium to the benefit of the insurance FOR YOU. A sizable premium and the benefits it produces might be thoroughly justifiable in your best friend's circumstances, but might not be at all appropriate in your situation.

2. As to the purchase of insurance by mail—

Is the company licensed in your state?

Are you satisfied as to the company's stability and performance record, especially as to claims? (a question you might well ask yourself about any insurance purchase, by mail or otherwise).

Does saving in premium or gain in benefit amount to enough to offset not having local agency service?

There are some very reliable companies which sell by mail. That they have policyholders who renew year after year attests to customer satisfaction. Other people prefer the availability of personal consultation and are willing to pay something for it if necessary.

3. Keeping an up-to-date inventory of possessions can prove to be very worthwhile in the event that the filing of a claim for loss becomes necessary. Some people do it by photographing such articles as lend themselves to photography, and listing the remainder. Others keep written lists. The method is not important; the maintaining of a current list is. The updating should include reasonably current appraisals where necessary, e.g., jewelry, silverware, etc.

4. Think well about the limits of liability which are best for you in your automobile insurance. A wise counselor of mine said to me shortly after I had started in business, "Don't settle for whatever your state requires as minimum liability

coverage. All you have to do is hit one bus loaded with children on their way to a picnic, and whether or not you are liable you'll have enough lawsuits on your hands to break you.'' The premium difference between whatever your state's minimum liability coverage is and, for instance, $100,000/$300,000 (bodily injury per person/per accident) is not very much. A reading of what some of the awards in liability cases nowadays amount to will convince you that this type of additional coverage is well worth the premium.

5. Think about who beside yourself should know where your insurance policies and records are kept. During the very week in which this is being written, a neighbor of ours suffered a stroke. She lives alone. Fortunately, when it happened she was in the driveway, and a friend saw her, and was able to have her rushed to the hospital. She cannot speak, and she is partly paralyzed.

Her daughter thinks, "She has some kind of insurance." The daughter does not know if the coverage is with a commercial carrier or if it is with Blue Cross. She does not know where her mother's records are or where the policy or policies are.

Enough said. It is always a good idea to make sure that someone who would be among the first to know if sudden illness or disability strikes you has knowledge of where information regarding your insurance may be found.

6. If ever you have occasion to compare one policy with another, make certain to compare coverages, limits, exclusions, and riders as well as premiums. A superficial comparison may result in an erroneous conclusion.

7. Try to look ahead to future needs, not just to today's.

Questions on Chapter Three

1. Why is adequate insurance important?

2. What are two basic rules to follow?

3. What are some of the reasons other than the costs of death for owning life insurance?

4. What are two or three commonly owned types of life insurance?

5. An annuity serves what purpose?

6. What is meant by "group insurance?"

7. What are some of the major hazards of home and automobile against which to insure?

8. What is the maximum advisable time period between reviews of your insurance?

9. What are some of the special considerations to think about—and to act upon?

IV
Investing

Investment aims—Government securities— Stocks—Corporate bonds—Municipal bonds —Mutual funds—Closed-end funds—Money Market funds—Investment clubs—Final thoughts.

After Savings, What?

The bank accounts have been established. At least the minimum previously suggested is in the savings account. Adequate insurance is in force. There is still some money to be put aside. So, now what?

Course One would be to build the savings a bit more. You might feel that you want a fatter cushion for unknown emergencies, or for just plain wants. If so, fine. Now, however, we will assume that if that had been your initial decision, it, too, has been accomplished. In either case it is time for the next step.

Course Two is that of investing. Where? What? How?

The initial move in developing a sound investment program is the same as that stated in the beginning of the book: determine objectives.

Two examples will show why this is the case. The first is that of a good friend of mine, a highly successful surgeon. About forty years of age, alert to his professional growth, he has enough of a problem in finding time for reading and study related to his specialty, let alone following the investment markets. What should he do?

"You aren't interested in income, are you?" I asked him.

"Huh! I couldn't care less about more income at this stage of the game. Taxes would take too much of it anyway. What I want is some reasonably solid growth so that when I decide to call it quits, perhaps in twenty years, I will be comfortably fixed."

He has been shaping his plans accordingly.

Contrast that case to that of the recently widowed woman who is just a couple of years older than my doctor friend. She had two children in college and a comfortable home to maintain. There was some income from money from insurance, a monthly income which would last for several years resulting from an agreement between her husband and his partner so that the survivor could buy out the share of the first of them to die, a few securities, and some cash. She needed all of that income. How should she invest?

Her interest was in getting all the income possible. She could use it for college bills. Growth of her investments was of no particular concern at the moment. Later, maybe. She might or might not remarry someday. If later on the need for income was reduced, then the portfolio could be rearranged.

You may not be at either of these extremes as to income vs. growth. You may be somewhere in between. It would be well to determine that to your own satisfaction before jumping into or out of an investment program.

U.S. Government Securities

It is arguable as to whether or not some U.S. securities should be classified as savings rather than investments. By the very name of some of them they seem to fall into the savings category. Since our purposes are not those of arguing definitions, let us treat these government issues right here, after the comments on savings and before we come to the subject of various forms of investments.

United States Savings Bonds, the E bonds, are so well known they probably need no more than a once-over-lightly touch.

They may be bought in a number of denominations ranging upward of $25. They are bought at a discount, with the interest accruing in six-month increments to the date of maturity. It is important to note that the interest is not on a straightline increase, i.e., if you surrender the bond prior to maturity the interest accumulated to the date of the early redemption will not be at as high a rate as it ultimately would have been had the bond been retained to maturity.

Furthermore, the interest accrues only at six-month intervals, so any redemption prior to maturity earns interest only to the end of the previous six-month interest date.

Interest is taxable income, but there is a choice in reporting it. It may be reported as it accrues, or the tax may be deferred to the maturity date or earlier redemption date.

In 1973 an increase in interest was granted on outstanding bonds, so if you own any which were in original or extended period in December of that year you have been the recipient of the new rate.

H bonds are current income bonds which pay interest every six months. The holder receives the interest; it does not accrue, as in the case of E bonds.

E bonds may be exchanged for H bonds in a minimum amount of $500. (Note, however, what was said about interest being credited to an E bond at six-month intervals. If you consider an exchange from E bonds to H try to arrange it at, or shortly after, the interest adjustment date of the E bond so that you do not lose a long period of interest.)

There are many rules about ownership, beneficiary, titling, and other aspects of these bonds. Here are a couple of them.

An E bond cannot be assigned. That is, for example, you could not put up some of your E bonds as collateral for a loan.

In the case of an H bond with co-owners the checks will go to the first named co-owner at the address shown on the bond. The checks would show the names of both, but could be cashed by either.

Your banker can give you complete information about E and H bonds. If you seriously consider a purchase of either of these types of government securities, it would be well to ascertain the rules pertaining to what you contemplate in terms of ownership, beneficiary, and so forth.

TREASURY BILLS. These are short-term government obligations. The minimum amount for purchase is $10,000. Interest return is for the duration of the bill, but the rates which bills pay fluctuates from time to time with the conditions of the money market. Since they are issued for periods of three, six, nine, or twelve months they are bought by many people as temporary depositories for money between other investments, or until such time as the investor wants his money for whatever purpose. There is an active market for them, so they can be bought and sold at any time.

Your banker, or a broker who handles government securities is your simplest source of purchase. You may, however, buy directly from a Federal Reserve bank.

TREASURY NOTES. Most may be bought in a minimum amount of $1,000, though there are exceptions.* The notes run for different periods longer than those of the bills. They may be issued in registered form, i.e. in the owner's name or, non-registered in coupon form. If you decide to register a note you may expect some delay in receiving the note, and again a delay of perhaps a couple of weeks in receiving your check if you sell. The reason is the registering process at purchase, and the proper clearance and verification procedures when you sell.

Your banker or a dealer in government securities can buy the notes for you for a small fee.

Government securities of the above types have the backing of the government, and are given a top rating for safety of principal. The E and H bonds are convenient as to amounts available and ease of purchase. They require no fee or service charge. Other issues of the government and instrumentalities of government are available too.

Lending to Individuals

Please see chapter on Lending and Borrowing.

---

*It is not usually practical for the purchaser to buy less than $5,000 or $10,000 as purchase costs reduce the net yield disproportionately on smaller amounts.

Stocks

When you acquire a share of stock you become part-owner of the business. A stock certificate represents equity, a share of ownership. If there are 5,000 shares of stock outstanding and you own 100 you are a 1/50 owner of the company.

The value of a stock is not a constant. It will rise and fall with the earnings of the business, economic conditions, worth of the business, conditions peculiar to the particular type of business, market conditions, and other factors.

Most corporations (exceptions being such as certain types of financial businesses) do not pay out all they earn. Some of the earnings are retained to plow back into the business. The dividend which the stockholder receives is dependent upon earnings, but also upon what the directors of the company feel should be retained for use by the corporation, for surplus (the financial cushion), for what they contemplate to be future needs, or for other reasons.

Many companies have paid dividends every year for decades, but that does not mean the dividends have always been in the same amounts. If it is your decision that you need a fixed amount of income from your investments, that you ought not hazard the possibility of a passed dividend (no dividend being paid for a particular period), then perhaps you should look at other types of investments, or at least limit your consideration of stocks to those with long, consistent dividend records. The growth stock typically pays a much smaller dividend because relatively more money is being plowed back into the business—the very process which makes for growth. The income type of stock normally does not have quite the growth potential as is anticipated for the so-called growth stock. There are other reasons for anticipating growth, however. These include new inventions which may open whole new markets, revolutionary changes in old products, designs, or services, and well-established company policies of ever-moving forward in research and development. If the growth stock performs as is hoped, it will be worth more as time goes on, the attractive feature for those who, like my doctor friend mentioned above, do not need the income now.

Before we leave this brief and very general discussion of stocks, I should touch upon the significance of a few of the terms applied to stocks.

Common stock represents equity or ownership of the corporation. If the company is dissolved, and all obligations, debts and bills are paid, the remaining assets belong to the common stockholders. *Preferred stock* is stock which has preference of some sort, usually in regard to being assured of a fixed rate of dividend. For instance, the dividend on the common stock may be reduced or even passed, but the obligation for the preferred stock dividend remains. If for reasons of extreme financial stringency a preferred dividend is not paid, usually the terms call for payment of dividends which are in arrears prior to, or concurrent with resumed payments of dividends on the common stock.

The advantage of the preferred stock is that there is a known amount of return, and that with preference over the common. The disadvantage is that it is not likely to have the degree of upward movement in price, regardless of how well the company does, whereas the common stock may appreciate greatly with good corporate financial results.

Sometimes in an effort to "sweeten" the preferred issue in regard to the aspect just mentioned, a *conversion* clause is included. It provides that the preferred may be converted into common on the ratio of so many shares of common for each share of preferred. This has the advantage to the holder of the preferred that IF the common reaches a market price which would put the owner of the preferred ahead of the game by making the conversion, he or she may take advantage of the clause and exchange the preferred for common.

Buying and Selling

Marketability of an investment is a desirable attribute. This applies to other investments as well as to stocks.

I once owned some stock in a small corporation which a dozen of us had formed to begin a new business venture. It would have been almost impossible to sell that stock had I wished to do so. Who would have bought it? We had no earnings record, few tangible assets, and we were just creating a market.

Stockholders of thousands of small businesses, many of them family owned, would find their shares subject to very limited marketability. The business may be very profitable, but that does not mean the stock is readily marketable.

I think of a successful, family operated music store in a small Pennsylvania town. Would you be interested in buying into it if you could? Of course not. Where would you ever be able to sell the stock if you wished to dispose of it?

All of this is not to say that one should never acquire stock in a closely held company. It is to say that one should consider the degree of importance of a reasonably quick sale in the event disposition of the stock is desired.

Stocks which are listed on the various stock exchanges offer no problem in this regard. Stock markets are just that: market places for the buying and selling of stocks, and purchases and sales may be made readily through brokerage firms. In the case of unlisted securities you may or may not be able to find a representative of one of the investment houses to assist you. That depends upon different factors, but you may find that you are pretty much on your own.

Are Stocks for You?

Are stocks for you? I can give you a quotation variously attributed to Socrates, Solon, and others, "Know thyself." Among the considerations you should weigh is this one, "Am I psychologically adaptable to the ups and downs of the market?"

This story is illustrative. I sat with some good friends who, for their situation, were fairly heavily invested in stocks. The beginning of some weakening in the general economy had been showing. The stock market had been sliding off. The value of their portfolio had dropped by a few thousand dollars.

The husband took the position that perhaps the market would go down quite a bit more, but that it would come back sooner or later. The wife said that she lay awake at night worrying about what would happen to their investments and to their income. She was beginning to have stomach distress from worry and concern. They asked what I thought they should do.

I responded that I thought the husband's appraisal correct, but that if the concern was that grievous for the wife, they should get out of the market, and put their money into something such as government securities, certificates of deposit, or something of that sort.

"That's the same thing our broker told us," said the husband.

On the other hand, I once had a client who had invested in stocks for many years. When she retired she had a portfolio worth far more than she had put into it and at the same time provided her with a good income.

Best advice before jumping very deeply into stocks: have a thorough talk with your investment adviser or broker, and be sure to have some discussion with him or her about the disadvantages as well as the advantages of stock ownership.

Corporate Bonds

A bond is an evidence of indebtedness. When you buy a corporate bond you become a creditor of the corporation. Payment of interest to you is a corporate obligation. It is not dependent upon the earning of a profit during a particular year or interest period. Whatever the interest stated in your bond is what you will receive, usually on a semi-annual basis. If the corporation is liquidated you will be paid before the stockholders. Corporate bonds are normally issued in a minimum amount of $1,000, and in multiples thereof, but this is not always the case.

As in the case of stock prices, bond prices are subject to change. If you hold a bond which pays six-percent interest, but conditions have changed to the extent that new borrowers are willing to pay eight-percent for loans based on similar quality bonds, then you are not likely to get the face amount of your bond if you sell it. Of course, if interest rates go the other way you may make a gain. As a general rule, however, the bond market is not quite as volatile as the stock market. Fluctuations tend to respond to interest rates.

Some corporations are more financially stable than others. A borrowing firm which is less secure will have to pay a higher rate of interest to attract money than would a more stable borrower, all else being equal.

One general rule is: the more speculative the investment the higher the rate of return (also the higher the risk).

Another general rule is: the longer the period to maturity, the higher the rate of return. (The buyer demands higher interest because inflation is likely to erode the buying power of his interest.)

There are numerous types of corporate bonds, and since this is not a textbook on stocks and bonds we will confine ourselves to descriptions of a few of the more common bond terms.

The *debenture* bond is simply a general obligation bond. It is supported by no special asset, but by the corporation's promise and ability to pay.

As a contrasting example, a *mortgage* bond is guaranteed by the pledge of some particular parcel/s of ground or buildings as collateral.

A *convertible* bond is one which may be converted into stock on some basis stated in the bond.

A *callable* bond is one which may be redeemed (called) by the issuer, usually after some specified time.

A *sinking fund* bond is one for the payment of which a special fund is created and gradually built to provide money for redemption. Sinking fund bonds are often callable so that the issue may be retired gradually rather than waiting for the maturity date to redeem the entire issue.

This is by no means a complete list of descriptions, but it does point out various bond features, and hence the need for a purchaser to recognize the terms of the money being loaned in exchange for a bond.

Most brokerage offices have numerous compendiums, reports, stock and bond rating services, and their own, or other, research reports available. Annual reports to stockholders may be secured directly from corporate headquarters. These can be helpful in your evaluation of a company in which you think you may be interested. Aside from statements of operations, earnings, new developments, etc., there will be included, probably in the auditor's notes, other important information such as what unfunded pension plan obligations exist, and what major lawsuits are pending.

I think of some women of my acquaintance who are quite knowledgeable about investments. Most of them do not try to "go it alone." They rely upon their advisers for assistance and guidance.

Municipal Bonds

A municipal bond is issued by a governmental or quasi-governmental body such as a city, a school district, a sewer authority, or a turnpike authority. There are numerous such bodies which have occasion to borrow money through bonds from time to time.

One distinguishing characteristic of municipal bonds is that the interest they pay is free from federal income tax. This feature makes them attractive to people in high tax brackets. A taxpayer whose top bracket is 40 percent who holds a corporate bond paying 9 percent has a return of 5.4 percent after federal income tax. Had the same individual bought a 6 percent tax exempt municipal bond the entire 6 percent return would still be left after federal income tax. All of this is without any consideration of possible state tax exemption.

Municipals, generally speaking, have had a good performance record. Like corporate bonds, they are somewhat less actively traded than stocks. Also, like corporate bonds, they are issued for varying lengths of time to maturity.

* * * * *

If you like fixed income, are not especially concerned about growth of investments, or about trying to beat inflation through your choices, then you well may wish to think about adding some bonds to your portfolio. Here again we go back to Chapter One: what are your objectives? If bonds seem to fit into them perhaps it would then be time to put your adviser to work checking out some possibilities for you.

Funds of Various Sorts

MUTUAL FUNDS. A mutual fund is a company that invests, for example, in the stocks of other companies. The mutual fund buyer would then own his pro-rata share of all such investments.

I have before me the prospectus of a mutual fund. It states that the particular fund is a "diversified open-end management investment company."

It is "diversified" as to its holdings. It does not restrict investments to any one industry or group of such, as do some funds. Also, the purpose of the fund is stated to be primarily that of growth, but with some regard for current income as well.

"Open-end" means that the fund will redeem shares at any time upon request of a shareholder. The fund secures its money from investing through the sale of new shares or from gains made from the sales of securities already owned.

"Management investment" indicates that the fund employs an investment adviser and manager to advise and manage, serve the fund with necessary research, and so forth. Often the term used is "investment management."

This is a typical mutual fund structure.

The fund earns money through dividends (sometimes interest) on its investments, and through gains made upon the sale of some of the fund's holdings. The shareholder participates in these earnings through dividends which may be taken in cash or reinvested. Like other securities, the value of a share rises and falls, but even so, many women find in mutual funds advantages they like: professional management, diversification, and ready marketability (redemption of shares by the fund, which is customarily made without charge).

There are three ways to make money in a mutual fund:

1. Dividends paid to the fund are generally passed along to the fund owner. He or she may take them in cash or reinvest them in the fund.

2. When the fund buys and sells stocks it frequently makes a profit. These capital gains are passed along.

3. If the value of a fund's investments goes up it will be reflected by an increase in the market price.

Not all funds—there are literally dozens of them—perform equally well. Some do very well; some do poorly. It pays to look at a fund's past performance record, though even that is no guarantee of what the future will hold. Some mutual funds make a sales charge at the time of purchase; some do not.

The ones which do not are the "no-load" funds. There appears to be no correlation between whether or not a fund is a "load" or a "no-load" and the results achieved. A charge, of course, has to be made against the fund for investment and management services performed, and this is true whether these services are performed by fund personnel or by outside investment counsel.

CLOSED-END FUND. This type of fund issues shares in certain blocks from time to time. It is not open to purchase once the currently authorized shares have been sold. The closed-end fund does not redeem its shares as does the mutual fund, but marketability is provided, at least in the instances of the larger funds through usual stock market channels. These funds provide diversification and management expertise just as do the mutual funds.

MONEY MARKET FUNDS. These funds are invested in relatively short-term obligations such as government securities, certificates of deposit, commercial paper (notes of corporations), and notes or debentures of banks or other financial institutions. The mechanics of operation are somewhat similar to those of other funds. Some funds make a sales charge; some do not.

These funds, dealing as they do in large amounts of money, usually are able to earn somewhat higher interest rates than most of us, as individuals, could hope for. They are not meant to be growth oriented, but rather they strive for high yields.

The minimum amount required to buy into the

fund varies, but in most cases it is conveniently small enough for anyone interested in this type of investment.

At the other end of the line, there are convenient arrangements for total or partial withdrawals. Fund management, of course, makes a charge for its services.

There are dozens of money market funds. Inquiry to any of them will bring descriptive matter.

Real Estate (as investment)

Please see chapter on Real Estate.

Investment Clubs

An investment club consists of a group of people, men, women, or mixed membership, each of whom puts in a certain amount of money per month. The club members discuss what investments they might wish to make, decide upon them, and do the same in regard to selling present holdings. Meetings usually are held at least monthly, though they may be more frequent.

A club is likely to have an investment adviser who may or may not attend meetings. Members find a certain social, as well as proprietary interest in their clubs. Generally, monthly invested sums are not large, and normally a club will buy the interest of a member who resigns from the club.

Some clubs are rather conservative in their policies and choices of investments; others are "go-go" oriented. Some have done well over a period of time; others have not fared very well. If you are invited to join an investment club you will be rewarded for taking the time and effort to look at the record, look at the policies, look at the present members. You will be happier with your decision, whichever way it goes, if you do.

Other Investments

Other investment possibilities do exist. Many of them call for real expertise, or at least complete confidence in the person who possesses that expertise. There may be, for instance, opportunities to join in some small business venture, or to buy a share in some oil rights. (Are they investments or speculations?) There are ventures and propositions which may be safe enough but offer small returns, and others which project fanciful returns but which likely are not so safe.

Then, too, there are means of simply releasing the responsibilities of selection and management of investment to others. Some women rely upon one of the investment management services. These may be local, or they may be national in scope. Announcements and advertisements in the financial pages, or in the case of the large services in financial magazines and papers will give you some leads. Other women are quite happy with having chosen the living trust (to be discussed in a subsequent chapter). Some rely solely on the recommendations of their investment advisers.

Any of these methods may prove to be quite the best for any one person, but they are not, per se, investments. They result from the election not to handle the management and responsibilities of investment yourself. For many people that is a good decision.

—And You?

What is best for you? There is no one correct answer. It depends upon:

What your objectives are,

What sorts of investments appeal to you, or interest you,

What investments would you feel comfortable in holding—comfortable in the sense of not fretting, feeling secure, feeling that you have made the best choice for YOU.

And, finally, in the event that you have had any doubts, have you checked your opinions with a qualified adviser?

Questions on Chapter Four

1. What should the very first move in developing an investment program be?

2. How does a government H bond differ from an E bond?

3. How does a treasury note differ from a treasury bill?

4. A share of stock represents what?

5. Is the income of any stock at a fixed rate?

6. How is a growth stock likely to differ from an income stock?

7. Corporate bonds are evidences of what?

8. What major difference is there between corporate bonds and municipal bonds?

9. What is meant by the term "convertible" as applied to certain types of stocks or bonds?

10. What is the difference between a mutual fund and a closed-end fund?

11. What is a money market fund?

12. If you just "don't want to be bothered" with caring for your investments what are some avenues you might consider?

V
Real Estate

Owning your residence—Usual reasons—Some
fallacies—Other reasons—Accentuation in real
estate investments—Advantages and disadvantages—Cooperatives and Condominiums—
Mortgages and sales agreements.

Some Initial Observations

This chapter begins with a conclusion which I have
reached from many observations over the years. I
cannot validate it with statistics. I would not even
argue the point with someone who does not agree. It
is extremely doubtful that any survey or study could
be comprehensive enough to confirm my conclusion,
or negate it.

Whether or not it is as generally true, as I believe it
to be, really does not make much difference, because
regardless of the extent of its validity, it makes a
significant starting point for our consideration of
real estate as an investment.

I have observed that people seem to do very well, indeed, in their real estate investments or else they do not do very well at all. Middle ground does not seem to be typical.

To some extent this may be due to happenstance, but in a number of cases it is probably due to reasonably ascertainable causes, as you will see from some of the examples which follow.

Our considerations will be divided between ownerships of property used as your own, or family residence, and property owned solely for investment purposes. We will then take a look at some special forms of ownership and some other types of real estate investments besides the usual outright property ownership.

Residence Ownership

Home ownership is a good idea for those who can afford it, and who do not object to the responsibilities of owning property. However, I think it is a good idea for reasons quite different from the ones often suggested.

The usual ones include: "It is one way to be sure to keep pace with inflation," "All that money for rent! I'd rather put it in a house," and "If it doesn't work out, or I don't like it, I can always sell the place."

I am sure you have heard these reasons or

variations of them more than once. Let us examine them briefly before we go on to what I think are much better reasons.

First of all, there is the one about keeping pace with inflation, always increasing in value, etc. Here are some cases in various parts of the country involving residential properties with which I am familiar. In all instances the homes were—and with one exception still are—in good, middle class neighborhoods. As far as I know all prices paid were commensurate with going values, and, obviously the sale prices were acceptable. The gain or loss figures are approximate as I have tried to adjust costs for improvements made, and I do not have figures for sales commissions in all cases where commissions were paid. If the gain or loss shown is off by a few percentage points, it really does not matter for the purpose involved. The fact to be established is that one does not always win—inflation or not.

Areas	*Years owned*	*Percentage Gain (G) or Loss (L)*
	37	16L
Examples are located	3	12G
in New England,	3	15L
mid-west, mid-east,	9	12G
and south. All urban	7	30G
or suburban — no	5	16L
rural properties	4	20G
	4	No G; No L

The next often suggested reason for owning is, "It is cheaper than renting." I doubt that would be subscribed to by the ones with the losses shown above. Be that as it may, here are some figures which are as close to accurate as I can make them. We will use the no-gain-no-loss property shown above so there will be no room for argument about "yes, but what about increase or decrease in property value?"

An item which must not be overlooked in making evaluation of owning vs. renting is the value of the money tied up in owned property. If the money were not invested in that property it would be available for other investments. In our examples we will assume that it could be earning six percent. Here are the figures.

Value of property—$52,000	
which @ 6% would otherwise	
produce income of	$3120
Taxes	1100
Insurance (basic only)	200
Maintenance (excl. cost of yard service) and Repairs	400
Water, misc.	150
	$4970

Note: Taxes have gone up again since the time of these figures; in comparison with rent—depending upon terms of lease—cost of heat might have to be added to above if heat would be furnished in the rental property; above figures for maintenance and repairs are probably inadequate to cover the once-in-20-to-25-year cost for furnace replacement, new roof, etc.

That is over $400 per month, which at the time of

the above figures would have rented a nice house or apartment—and one would still have the $52,000 instead of the house.

Admittedly, one can make counter arguments such as to the effect that taxes and interest on the mortgage are deductible items while the income from the $52,000 otherwise invested would not be. And it can be argued that one would not likely have as much floor space in the property rented for the $400 per month. All right, but then what about the other side of that coin? We did not show any cost of lawn service. Forget hiring someone. What about fertilizers, treating for insects, spending money for nursery items and care? What about all the little items which one would require for owned-property use that one would not likely have to the same extent for rental property use: tools, equipment, possibly appliances. Also the $400 maintenance figure is conservative as to major items such as those indicated in the note below the figures.

Not to labor the point, let us assume that there is a difference of a couple of hundred dollars a year in favor of owning largely due to the deductible interest and taxes. That is a far cry from "All that money going for rent! I'd rather put it in a house." The fact is that monthly payments include interest, and depending upon arrangements with the lender, perhaps amounts to be escrowed for taxes and insurance. The payments are not all put into equity in the house. What probably happens is that the owner puts more into the house than would be put into rental property, but equates it with being a similar amount.

How about the last of the oft-given reasons, "If it doesn't work out, or I don't like it, I can always sell it."

There is an old adage with real estate professionals to the effect that every house has its buyer. Except for completely deteriorated houses, condemned houses, etc., the statement is probably true. Sometimes the problem is: when will the buyer be found, and what price will the property bring? Twice my wife and I had to finance two residences for several months until the buyers were found.

Right now we have some friends, a professional man and his wife, who bought a new home about six months ago. They still have not sold their former residence, and they are beginning to feel the pinch.

Yes, if you decide to sell the property you own you can do it, but do not count on doing it the day after tomorrow.

So why do I say that ownership is a good idea if there is not a large difference in dollars? For those willing to accept ownership responsibilities there are a number of good reasons.

1. You cannot be dispossessed by the landlord. During our early married years my wife and I rented a pleasant little house. We lived there for about three years and would have liked to stay for another couple until we were prepared to buy or build our own place. The landlord's daughter was about to be married, and she, too, liked the house. Result: we were given

notice to vacate. Perfectly legal. Perfectly understandable. But that did not help us.

2. You can do what you want within building code and zoning restrictions. We have a friend who is really a plant lover. She has a greenhouse built immediately adjacent to the study in her home. Can you imagine many landlords who would sanction that?

3. It is not unreasonable to hope that inflation will help to offset depreciation of your property, although as you have seen above, it does not always work out that way. Other factors are sometimes more significant, and they are not always controllable. Nevertheless, in many cases, the hope materializes.

4. You may decorate, alter, paint, remodel to your own taste. Landlords are not always agreeable to that. We once rented from a man who wanted only one of two colors on the walls. He believed that any others might require a paint job to please subsequent tenants should we move.

5. Ownership provides the security of having a home base, a feeling of "This I have; they can't take it away from me." This kind of satisfaction can be worth a great deal, regardless of whether or not you are really saving much money by owning.

If you are willing to wrestle with the upkeep, maintenance and occasional emergency problems instead of relaying them to a landlord, go to it. In that case you will probably be happy in your home ownership. Possibly you will make some money far down the way when you sell. But again you may not, as you have seen above, so please do not acquire that home solely on the premise that it will earn a handsome return for you. It may. We can hope so.

Please be sure to read the section "Before you sign—," which follows later in the chapter.

Investment Ownership

At the beginning of the chapter, there was reference to the likelihood of doing very well or not well at all with real estate investments. When we talk of utilizing real estate as an investment medium we come full face to that observation.

Undoubtedly some readers, and almost surely some real estate experts, would say, "Sure, but isn't the same thing true of people who make other kinds of investments?" To this I reply, "Yes, but——."

And it is a great big "BUT." "Yes, but real estate tends to accentuate the likelihood more so than other investments." There are two reasons for this being the case.

First of all is the simple matter of diversification. If you have $25,000 to invest and you put it into stocks, or bonds, or mutual funds, or even your little investment club, you will have some spread of risk.

You would probably have at least a half dozen stocks or bonds not all of which will go away up or away down. If you buy two or three or even only one mutual fund you will have built-in diversification. If, however, you buy real estate you will probably acquire just one parcel. Your gain or loss will be dependent solely on its performance. Even if you spread yourself thin enough to buy two properties you will not have much diversification, especially if the properties are similar, closely located to each other, or of the same general type.

The second way in which real estate is likely to accentuate gain or loss is in the leverage exercised by mortgaging the property.

If in the example above you used your $25,000 as a down payment on a building and obligated yourself for a mortgage of $75,000, you would then be dealing with a $100,000 piece of property. Eventually, if when you sell it you have a ten percent gain or a ten percent loss, the figure would be $10,000, not $2,500—quite an accentuation.

For some people these accentuations are perfectly all right. The question is: are you one of those people? Back to Chapter One: What are your objectives? What are you trying to accomplish? If the answers to these questions make real estate an appropriate investment for you, the next question is similar to the one asked about stocks. "Am I psychologically adaptable to owning real estate?" Then it is time to appraise your own knowledge and/or the availability of qualified expert knowledge to enable you to carry through successfully.

There are advantages and disadvantages. Here are some with actual case examples.

Advantages

I have a friend whose experience well points up some important advantages.

Over a period of time he has acquired six or seven houses in the same neighborhood solely as an investment. So far he has capitalized on some of the normal advantages, and the chances are that he will continue to do so.

1. Steady income. He keeps the houses rented and his tenants satisfied through proper care and maintenance.

2. Capital appreciation. To date it appears that should he want to sell any or all of the properties he would be ahead of the game.

3. Inflation hedge. Much the same as "2" above.

4. Retirement income. Long before he is ready to retire the mortgages will be paid (paid by insurance if he dies prematurely), so his net income will be clear during his later years, or for his family if he dies before paying off the mortgages.

Now let us look at him as a candidate for real estate investment. He is a long-time resident of his city. He knows real estate. He is an executive of a large local business. He has almost no likelihood of moving from the city. His business is related to the building trades. He is a "natural" for real estate investing.

A similar investment for another executive of the same age and with the same amount of money, but who is highly subject to transfer, who does not know the city, or local trends and conditions, and who knows or cares little about real estate would be a disaster.

Disadvantages

Take the case of another friend, an older professional man who understands the arithmetic, the legal implications, the taxes, and is perfectly willing to pay for hired property management.

He owns an apartment building which he bought some years ago. The location is in a large eastern city. The neighborhood has deteriorated to some extent. Security has become a problem. He has no luck with finding good building superintendents even though he is perfectly willing to pay a reasonable salary. The taxes keep climbing with no end in sight. He cannot keep rental income in line with costs, and his margin is approaching a mere break-even point. Why doesn't he sell? He would be delighted to do so except that under present conditions he would have to sell at a considerable loss.

His case typifies some disadvantages that can occur.

1. Deteriorating neighborhood—completely beyond his control. I think of another situation in another city where there is a strong effort to have the zoning ordinance changed in a middle class residential district. The property owners are fighting the proposal but they may not win. If they do not their property values almost surely will suffer.

2. Headaches. If there is no real estate management, or building manager or even if there is a poor one, who gets the grief? The building owner.

3. Non-liquidity. If funds are needed, really needed, can the owner raise them on the property? Maybe. Maybe not. It depends upon the size of the mortgage and many other factors. My friend's apartment house represents about one-fourth of his estate. Add to that the value of his home and other nonliquid assets, and his estate might be short of liquid funds.

   This borders on the "real estate poor" classification. I had a client once whose real estate holdings on paper showed $3,000,000, yet he told me he could not pry loose enough money to buy a small boat he would have liked to own. That is the extreme, of course, but a fair degree of liquidity is important.

4. The possibility of capital loss, as well as the

possibility of capital gain. True of other investments, the fact should not be ignored in real estate.

What has been said above about advantages and disadvantages of developed property, except for the problems of management, is largely true of undeveloped property.

I happen to be writing this chapter at a water's edge location at the seashore. The third lot from here was sold under unanticipated circumstances a year ago. The advantages came into play. But as I look out the window across the street, another lot still has a "For Sale" sign put up almost a year ago. I do not know who the owner is but if she or he needs the money, or wants to avoid paying taxes, then the disadvantage evidences itself.

Before You Sign

Whether your contemplated purchase of real estate is for your own residential usage or for purposes of investment you will protect yourself by asking these questions. If the answers are not favorable think well.

Is the price right? Once when I was about to make an offer for a house which appealed to my wife and to me as a residence, I followed my own advice.

I discussed the asking price, which I thought to be about right, with someone who was professionally involved in real estate, but not in the sales end of the business. He suggested that I offer 12-percent less than I had planned. I did not get the property at that figure, but I did get it for about five-percent less than I would otherwise have paid.

Is the basic construction sound? This is a crucial question, the answer to which required specialized knowledge of what to look for. If you are in doubt, it is worthwhile to pay a disinterested expert to give you an opinion. This can be a very important factor in considering investment property.

Is the condition sound? I recall one situation of a house in a nice neighborhood which was sold to new owners. Inside of a few months there was a suit filed against the previous owners for $10,000. The house was riddled by termites. In most parts of the country a termite check is a good thing to require.

In another recent case, a young couple bought a house only to find after they had moved in, when the first rain came, that the roof had numerous leaks.

Does the neighborhood show signs of deterioration or evidence of some disadvantage? Are there numerous "For Sale" signs in evidence? Are there a couple of houses or buildings vacant, or in poor repair?

If the property you contemplate buying is leased, how does the anticipated, or present rent compare with others nearby? What about vacancies in similar properties?

Right now I know of part of an office building which has been vacant for three years. The landlord turned down an offer of about 55 percent of what he had asked. Apparently he has badly misjudged "going rates," coupled with availability of other space and a somewhat deteriorating area.

What about taxes? The outlook for more and more increases? What will they do to rents you will have to charge?

It will pay to ask the questions and get the answers BEFORE YOU SIGN.

Other Forms of Ownership and Real Estate Investments

CO-OPERATIVE OWNERSHIP. Unde this form a group of people pool resources to acquire property. The co-op owns the property with each member having the rights to his or her individual unit or part. Changes to be made, and often even sale of an individual's unit to an outsider must be approved by the co-op. The body as a whole, usually through a board, works out plans for upkeep, building care, etc. In theory this relieves any one individual of routine care and maintenance other than small inside chores for the unit he or she occupies.

Problems can arise. I have one friend who owned a share in a very expensive co-op. There were eight members in all. Some of them wanted certain changes made in and about the apartment building.

Others opposed. At the time he told me about it something of a hassle was beginning to develop. Someone had to give in, or compromise must ensue.

The co-op has some advantages, but one disadvantage is that of not being one's own boss though in a sense one is his or her own landlord. Regardless of the size of your holding you have one vote.

CONDOMINIUM OWNERSHIP: One who buys a condominium, be it apartment, townhouse, or whatever, owns the unit bought. Financing is done on an individual basis and taxes are levied individually. The owner may sell, but sometimes it is required that the right of first choice of buying be given to the other owners.

Services outside the individual's own unit (care of trees and shrubbery on common grounds, snow removal, care of common walk ways, etc.) are provided for a monthly fee over and above any payments being made toward ownership of the particular unit.

Often the outside services are provided by the developer at first. Sometimes he continues to provide them; sometimes he relinquishes them to an association of the condominium owners. Sometimes fees remain as reasonable as can be expected; sometimes they are increased considerably.

Unlike the co-op, the condominium provides voice in matters of the total complex proportionate to the size of individual holding—not one vote regardless of size.

A couple of women I know are very pleased with their condominium ownership. They like the freedom from outside cares and maintenance. Not all experiences, however, are favorable. Some have found that the care and maintenance is not all that it should be, and some have been stunned by increasing service charges.

Best advice when considering either co-op or condominium: talk with those who already live there, check history of service fees, check history (if any) of re-sale possibilities, talk with your banker, and above all do not buy without your attorney's advice including his explanation of any of the contract terms you do not understand.

If you decide to buy, then, as in other real estate transactions, confer with your insurance adviser as to proper coverages.

MORTGAGES, SALES AGREEMENTS. These are not real estate investments, per se, but rather intangibles which are supported by real estate.

As investments they are as good as the people who commit themselves to pay the principal and interest and to the value of the real estate against which the obligations are issued.

The mortgage is a direct loan against the property. It is usually recorded at the court house, and it is a prime lien if it is a first mortgage. A second mortgage is a weaker investment as it is subsidiary to any first mortgage. Title passes to a new owner who is using mortgage money to acquire a property.

The sales agreement in at least one state known as a "land contract," provides for payment of principal and interest much as does a mortgage. The terms, however, are usually more restrictive with severe penalties for non-payment or delinquency.

The sales agreement is often used in cases in which the person buying property cannot make an adequate down payment to get a mortgage. Sometimes after enough payments have been made to provide reasonable equity the sales agreement is replaced by a mortgage. Title does not pass until the sales agreement has been fulfilled, or is replaced by a mortgage.

There are other more complex, and often more speculative plans and schemes for attracting money for various real estate ventures. If you are approached to participate, you would do well to check with your real estate adviser, your banker, and your attorney. If the offer is really attractive it can wait for the results of your investigative efforts.

Final Thought. The advice of a professional in the real estate business can be extremely valuable. Members of the National Association of Realtors (NAR) not only have the availability of study courses, but they also subscribe to the NAR's code of ethics.

Questions on Chapter Five

1. What are some of the usual reasons given in support of owning your own residence?

2. What are some of the fallacies?

3. What other reasons are encouraging for residential ownership?

4. For what two reasons are real estate investments likely to accentuate gains or losses as opposed to other forms of investments?

5. What are some advantages of investing in real estate?

6. Some disadvantages?

7. How does participation in a co-op differ from ownership of a condominium?

8. How does a sales agreement for a piece of property differ from a mortgage?

**You are now a little past the
half-way point.**

**This is a good place to pause, review,
and clear up any uncertainties.**

VI

Lending and Borrowing

Lending—Loans to family and friends—
Borrowing—Limits—Sources—Durations—
Repayment.

Taking and Making Loans

Of course, when you buy a government bond, or a corporate bond, or accept a mortgage for money you advance, you are lending. In this chapter, however, our considerations will be those of lending and borrowing at the *personal* level, with, or perhaps more often without, security for your loan.

Family Lending

First, we can almost dismiss family lending for the simple reason that usual rules and cautions do not apply.

Loans within the family—and that includes aunts,

uncles, cousins, in-laws—ordinarily are not made after careful review of financial statements, posting of adequate collateral, etc. Usually they are made for such purposes as: helping to fund college costs for someone's education, making money available for large, and perhaps unexpected hospital or medical bills, providing the down payment for a house being purchased by a family member, or for some unusual circumstance.

The appraisal usually is on the basis of "Do I want to help?" "Can I afford to help?" and "Is the request at least half-way reasonable?" If your answer to these questions is affirmative you will probably let that suffice, and then work out the terms.

Aside from the caution not to become the family's easy mark, there is only one rule that should be insisted upon in every case of family loans: Be sure that a written record, preferably in proper legal form is provided.

Because you expect to have to sue to collect? No. Because death or disability can strike you or the borrower.

Suppose you lend a favorite niece and her new husband money for the down payment on a house. A few months later the two of them are killed in an automobile accident. Just how would you be able to collect from either or both estates unless you held a note or a mortgage? No sensible executor or administrator would honor a claim just on your "say so."

Better yet, in addition to the note or other acknowledgement, ask for the assignment of life insurance in an amount to cover. When the loan is repaid the insurance can be turned back to the insured. It is simple. Your insurance adviser can guide you.

Above all, in the case of family loans, be sure there is proper written evidence thereof.

Personal Loans to Friends

Our text for this section is taken from Hamlet, Act One Scene Three. It is the oft-quoted advice of Polonius to Laertes:

> *Neither a borrower nor a lender be;*
> *For loan oft loses both itself and friend,*
> *And borrowing dulls the edge of husbandry.*

Shakespeare did not put these words into Polonius' mouth regarding loans to The King of Denmark or to The Elsinore Ferry Boat and Drayage Company. He was talking about loans to friends. After more than three hundred years the advice is still sound.

The best starting question for friends who want to borrow from you is, "Have you asked your banker about the idea, and for the money?" (There is a story later in the chapter about that.)

Banks are in the business of lending money. Their

money has to work to earn profit. They want to make loans—good loans. Your friend should start at his or her bank.

If the bank has said "no," then why should you be willing to take on the loan? Do you know something the banker does not? Is your experience in credit matters greater than the banker's? Your judgment better?

The simple truth is that if the banker said "no," then making the loan very likely would be a speculation and not an investment for you. This is doubly true if your friend has access to funds by using other assets of his or her own. (We will be looking at other sources of funds later in the chapter.)

If your friendship is so deep that you consider the friend to be "like one of the family," all right. Then make, or do not make the loan on the same emotional and personal considerations as we saw to be the ones applicable to family lending. Please be sure to recognize it for what it is, not as a true investment-type loan.

If your friendship is to stand or fall by your making or not making the loan, then do recall Laertes' admonition.

Loans to Strangers

Well, now - - - - - - - hm-m-m!!

Borrowing

Fortunate, indeed, are you if never you have to borrow—or perhaps not fortunate, but a bit too timid. There are times when proper borrowing is sensible. Like when? Like borrowing to do some remodelling because your mother is coming to live with you. Like borrowing to enable you to buy into a solid, growing business.

In any event, what sort of limits should be imposed on your borrowing? What sources are there? What durations of loans are reasonable?

Limits

The place to begin is with your own self-imposed limit. Early in the book we talked of budgets and expenses. If there is good cause for you to borrow, begin with a look at your budget and expense figures. How much leeway have you to pay back principal and interest while still maintaining some safe margin for emergencies?

I think of a tragic case of a young man about 19, married, wife not employed. He was earning about $5,000 a year. He had gone to his bank to try to arrange a loan to pay off all of his loans and work on repaying just one loan at the bank instead.

Now bankers and most other lenders take a dim view of "consolidation loans." Borrowers are usually already in trouble when they seek to do what the young man was attempting.

Imagine the banker's shock when he discovered that the total of the young man's debt was over $6,000. There was just no conceivable way that such an indebtedness could be cleared on his income. I do not know whatever happened to the poor fellow. I suppose bankruptcy eventually followed.

This financial horror story points up what can happen when budget and especially current expenses are disregarded in borrowing money.

If you approach your banker after you have decided that a loan for what you want would be sound, he or she will give your reasoning a thorough and worthwhile double checking.

Here is a perfect example. A friend and client of mine has a highly successful business. She has built a superb reputation, starting from scratch—a good enough reputation that she has been elected a director of a large national corporation.

A couple of years ago she had the idea of opening a second establishment to be of the same kind of business but in a different location, appealing to a different type of customer, utilizing different decor, etc.

By chance, at about the same time she was approached by two personable and articulate salesmen who convinced her of the merit of a new venture involving a product they had designed.

To go ahead on both projects she needed an initial $40,000. Her present establishment and home were completely clear. She approached her banker, a senior officer, who listened, reviewed, questioned, and discussed both propositions in detail.

Finally he said, "You know your credit is good with us. If you want $40,000, we'll lend it to you—BUT NOT ON THE BASIS OF THOSE PROPOSITIONS. I don't think either one is sound. You may have the money solely on the basis of your credit. Once you have it what you do with it is your decision. I do not recommend either of the proposals you have made, so if you proceed it is your decision and against my advice."

She went home and "slept on it." She decided that she was not the one to second guess or outsmart her banker. She dropped further considerations of both projects. Is she glad today that she did!!

This story illustrates that there are considerations of limits other than the sheer dollar limitations such as were wildly exceeded by the young man in the previous story. In the case of the woman above, she could have withstood a $40,000 loss, though with considerable trauma. Had she been thinking of putting $5,000 into those ventures it would not have mattered much to her whether everything worked out or not. Even at $40,000 the banker's concern obviously was not for her financial limit, but for limits prescribed by appropriateness and wisdom.

Sources

People often have available sources of funds which they do not think about, or do not want to consider. That friend, or family member, who wants to borrow $5,000 from you may have savings certificates, stocks, life insurance, or real property, which would serve as collateral for a loan—but it would be so much easier to get the money from you.

We looked at the lender's standpoint a few pages back. Now, let us reverse it. When you want to borrow be sure to search out all of your own available sources first.

Here briefly are some sources when you need to borrow.

BANK. Probably the best place to start. Remember the story about the woman who thought she wanted $40,000? Your banker will give you counsel as well as considering your request. The bank is in the business of lending money. Why not start there?

LIFE INSURANCE. Many years ago when I neither had much money, nor was making much money, we had acquired a property which we were having remodelled completely. Everything went wrong, including the contractor's running out of money and going broke. Suddenly I found that we needed about 25 percent more money than we had bargained for.

The property was already mortgaged so I certainly was not about to go back to my banker. We did not have the money in any bank accounts. I recall very well that it was near midnight. My wife and I very dejectedly were sitting wondering what to do. Then it dawned on me that my life insurance policies had loan values slightly in excess of what we needed. We were saved!

Advantages of the life insurance loan are ease of making (no questions asked), no schedule of repayment required, completely private, and probably a lower rate of interest than you can get elsewhere.

The disadvantages are similar. Perhaps the fact that it is easy to make induces you to borrow when you should not, or borrow more than you need. That there is no mandatory payback required makes it easy to put off, and off, and off repaying the loan. (Why not establish your own schedule and stick to it?) Finally, if you die with a policy loan outstanding the amount will be deducted from the total death benefit of the policy.

SAVINGS CERTIFICATES AND CERTIFICATES OF DEPOSIT. The mere fact that you hold one of these instruments which has a maturity date out in the future does not mean that if you need money you must redeem it and take the penalty for early redemption. Many institutions will lend you the amount of the certificate at perhaps one or one-and-a-half percent more interest than it is paying you. You repay the loan at maturity, or prior thereto.

For example, if you have such a certificate paying you six percent, you use it as collateral for a loan for which you will pay seven percent. You continue to get the six, so the net cost of your loan to you is one percent.

CREDIT UNION. If you belong to a credit union check the loan possibilities there. Terms are usually liberal, and credit unions are eager to serve their members.

SMALL LOAN COMPANIES (FINANCE COMPANIES). Their function is to make small loans, often of a non-bankable type. Interest rates are high. Rules for repayment are firm. This does not disparage their work. They serve a real purpose.

I recall once discussing with the president of a small loan company some of the problems of his business. He said, "People think we make a great deal of money because our interest rates are high. We don't. We do about as well on profit margins as other businesses. Our loans are small, and therefore, expensive to handle and administer. Collection costs are high. Defaults and delinquencies are real concerns. Not many of our customers are well-to-do people. We serve a purpose, and we try to do it well, but we don't get rich doing it, even with the interest rates we have to charge."

MORTGAGES. Real estate may be mortgaged, or if a mortgage already exists it may be increased. This process is usually time consuming, and not practical for short-term loans unless it is the only source.

A first mortgage is a prime lien against property. Many second mortgages are placed, too. A second is subordinate to the first on a property, so be prepared to pay a higher interest rate if you borrow money on a second mortgage.

SMALL BUSINESS ADMINISTRATION. If you need to borrow for purpose of starting or expanding a business you will do well to talk with the S.B.A. office near you. Much help is available without charge, whether or not a loan is made.

For example, S.B.A. provides the services of an organization known as SCORE (Service Corps of Retired Executives). Its members are retired executives who volunteer their services and expertise to people considering going into business as well as to those who already have established themselves in business, but who need help and counsel with some aspect of their business. This is a free source of valuable assistance.

If you are interested in borrowing money for business purposes the first place to go is to your bank.

1. If you are already in business take along your financial statements for the last year or two.

2. If you are contemplating going into business take along your projections of income and expense, along with your proposed budget.

Start with your banker. S.B.A. will answer questions, but will not consider either a loan guarantee or a direct loan (not much direct loan money is available) until they have evidence of your having been turned down by your bank. There are, however, some special arrangements for persons of minority groups.

Durations

Repayment time and schedule should fit the circumstances. One would not expect a car loan to run for seven or eight years. The car could be worn out, or worth little by then. Anyone needing that long would be overextended. A mortgage well may run for 20 years or more both because of amount of periodic payments required, and because there would be ample security throughout the period.

Perhaps no more than interest would be required for four years on a loan made to a college freshman. A loan to a senior should not have such generously delayed payments unless the borrower is going on to graduate school.

"Cut the cloth to fit the pattern." Try to be sure that there would be some salvageable cloth left if the garment is not paid for as scheduled.

Polonius received top billing in this chapter. Allow me the privilege of taking over the curtain lines.

It is so easy to dream up the reasons for borrowing; often it is easy to arrange the loan. Sometimes one borrows more than necessary, "just in case."

The lender hands over the check which is promptly put to intended uses. Then the tendency is to think, "That's that except for paying off the loan."

To quote from Hamlet once again, "Ay, there's the rub."

Money borrowed is not taxable income. It comes in at face value unless borrowed on a discount basis, i.e., with interest deducted in advance. But—

Money is repaid in after-tax dollars.

That is one fact which makes repayment of loans even more difficult than just scraping together payments in amounts to equal the loan. Oh, the interest on most types of loans is deductible, but that is not what the above statement refers to.

Let us say your loan is $10,000 and that your total income taxes (federal, state, city) total 25 percent of your income. You cannot deduct your repayments of loan principal. That means you must earn $13,333 in order to pay back your $10,000 loan.

——Ah, *"The slings and arrows of outrageous fortune!"*

Questions on Chapter Six

1. What considerations not present in public lending, such as in government bonds or corporate obligations come into play in loans to family members or friends?

2. Is borrowing almost always bad practice? Why or why not?

3. What could you tell a friend who asked your opinion on reasonable limits for a contemplated loan?

4. What are at least four possible sources of borrowing funds?

5. Is there a fixed relationship between type and/or size of loan and the duration for which it should be made? Explain.

6. What is one extremely important fact in the matter of repayment plans and calculations?

VII
The World of Trusts

Trusts and women—What is a trust—Types of
trusts: living, life insurance, testamentary—
Other personal trusts—Some purposes of trusts
—Related services—Pitfalls.

Trusts: Functions and Types

Some languages treat certain words denoting
inanimate objects male or female through the use of
a particular article or a special suffix. If English were
one of those languages I would suggest the female in-
dicator for the legal sense of the word "trust."

I venture the opinion that in most instances personal trusts are established primarily for the benefit
of females. I feel quite sure that of the millions of
dollars being paid from income and principal of
trusts actually under administration, most go to or
for the benefit of women rather than men. Today,
more and more women are establishing trusts of their
own, and more women are trust officers and ad-
ministrators than ever before. In short, trusts are im-

portant in the financial world of women and in their financial planning.

Mention "trust" and many listeners (male and female) begin to "tune out." That is unfortunate because the whole concept is really not overwhelmingly complex. The language and the technical mechanics can be fairly complex, but most persons are not concerned with how a trust is put together, or with why certain legal jargon is used. They are interested in what a trust can do and with what results are obtained.

What is a trust? It is a legal device whereby the creator, called "settlor" (under some circumstances "grantor" or "donor") places property of almost any kind (trust, estate or corpus) into the care of someone or some institution ("trustee") for the benefit of a person or persons ("beneficiary/ies") under terms spelled out in the trust document. The trustee is responsible for the care of the property held and for the proper distribution of both income and principal as directed by the provisions of the trust.

SETTLOR *property*→ TRUSTEE   *income*→ BENEFICIARIES
                   cares for   *and/or*
                   administers   *principal*
                   distributes   *as*
                                  provided

I can recall working with one trust of 18 legal-size pages. I have seen many trusts of only a couple of pages each. The substance of provisions depends upon what the settlor wants to accomplish. (Remember "Objectives?") Correct phraseology of necessary statements to achieve these ends is the attorney's concern. He must keep in mind clarity, tax consequences, possible contingencies, and conformity to legal requirements. Words and words.

Should everyone have a trust? No. Should many more people have trusts than do have them now? Equally emphatically, yes. You will see what some of the reasons are as we go along with numerous true-life examples, most of which involve women.

Clarity will best be served if first we look at some of the commonly used forms of trust, and then as we look at examples we can point up particular uses. These illustrative cases will show some of the reasons why people use trusts, and what circumstances make trusts desirable or even necessary. Then, too, we will look at some cautions and pitfalls.

The Living Trust

The living trust, which is also called an "inter vivos" trust, is established during the settlor's lifetime—hence its name. As with other trusts, the document spells out what is to be done with the trust property, also called "corpus," with the income it earns and what the terms are for distribution of the property, and when that is to take place.

It is not at all unusual for the initial income beneficiary of a living trust to be the settlor. You may recall the example in Chapter Four of the woman with two children in college whose concern was income, not growth. She does not consider herself an expert in managing investments, so she placed her holdings in a living trust with herself as the income beneficiary as long as she lives. She receives the benefit of professional management of her funds by the trust company which is trustee, while retaining the rights to both income and principal. At her death income will continue, or principal will be distributed depending upon circumstances at the time. The terms are all set forth in the instrument.

A living trust may be fully funded at the time it is established, or it may be partially funded with additions to be made to it as time goes on. It may even be a "dry" trust with little or nothing in it though it has been established to be ready to go into full operation later on.

The trust provisions will cover such matters as who is to decide about sales, purchases, or exchanges of investments, who is to determine investment policies and make the decisions, what the trustee's duties and powers are, and, of course, who the beneficiaries are to be, and what happens at the settlor's death. A very valuable provision is a "for benefit of" clause which permits the trustee to make payments for the benefit of a beneficiary. This can be most important to a beneficiary who is disabled or away for a long time.

The living trust affords relief from investment management whether the objectives are growth, income, or a combination of them. Along with that it affords a practical means of meeting problems such as some which will be typified later in the chapter. Sometimes a trust is the only means.

Another advantage of the living trust is that it by-passes probate, i.e., it is not settled under the terms of a will since it is already in being and its assets are already assigned their place in after-death retention or distribution. This means a smooth flow for the trust property, and likely the avoidance of probate costs other than taxes for the assets of the trust.

Furthermore, there is no publicity as to its terms, a fact which many persons consider to be a considerable advantage over a testamentary trust. You may read in the newspaper that Goldie Silverspoon left an estate estimated to be $300,000. You never will read that she left a living trust of $300,000 to be distributed thus and so.

Assuming the settlor of the trust has retained rights, then the value of the trust property will be subject to estate and inheritance taxes. The word "rights" applies not just to being able to say to the trustee, "I want some money for the trust." Much less than that may constitute "rights." It is a technical, legal point which, if encountered, should be discussed thoroughly with your attorney. The central point is that the living trust does not eliminate death taxes unless——and now comes the "unless."

Unless the trust is made *irrevocable* it will be part of the taxable estate. Irrevocable means "for keeps," not to be revoked, not to be subject to future changes of mind of the settlor.

The step of irrevocability is not to be taken lightly. In fact, it calls for counsel from your attorney, perhaps from your trust officer, and from your life insurance adviser if insurance is involved, and depending upon the property in the trust and your tax situation perhaps you should include your accountant.

The creating of an irrevocable trust may involve the making of a gift which throws the settlor face-to-face with gift taxes (to be discussed later). There are some situations in which irrevocable trust is a useful and desirable device, but those situations are in the minority. The irrevocability is final. It means just what it says.

One man decided several years ago that he was going to begin to divest himself of certain assets and put them into an irrevocable trust. His idea was to build it as time went on. He started it with a very modest amount.

He added nothing to it for a couple of years, and then decided he did not want to pursue that course. He attempted to retrieve the assets to put them to another use (whatever his idea happened to be at that time). The trust company said, "No." His attorney said, "No." Two more attorneys said, "No." So there sits his irrevocable trust with an absurdly small amount in it, and there it will stay until he dies.

Irrevocability: move cautiously and act only with advice of competent counsel.

Revocability is just what irrevocability is not. Revoke the trust. Amend it. Then amend it again. Do what you wish with it (within reason and legal limitations). Most living trusts are revocable. The competent counsel, and the proper drafting, and the technical requirements are all there, but not the "for keeps." It remains for the settlor to determine whether or not to retain it, or change it, or terminate it.

The Life Insurance Trust

This is a widely used form of trust, most commonly a living trust.

The primary assets are or will be life insurance policies or proceeds therefrom, but other assets may be deposited as well.

It may be revocable, as is usually the case, or it may be irrevocable.

The trustee may, or may not, hold the policies.

The trustee is named beneficiary of the policies. After the proceeds have been paid to the trustee then the trust operates under its terms just as in any other case.

This type of trust offers a flexibility and a degree of discretionary control not possible under the so-called "settlement options" of insurance companies.

The Testamentary Trust

Also known as "Trust Under a Will," the

testamentary trust is just that: a trust created by the last will or testament of an individual.

The testamentary trust is revocable. After all, it is a part of the will, and since a will can be destroyed or changed (we will talk about that later), then it follows that any trust which is part of that will may also be eliminated or changed.

Upon the death of the testator the trust under the will becomes irrevocable and final. That is the very purpose of the trust, to set forth what shall be done with the property directed to go into the trust, and when, and perhaps how. As in the case of the living trust, directions, details, discretionary powers, and other items are set forth.

Unlike the living trust, after the death of the creator of the testamentary trust its terms may be learned by the public.

After a will is filed for probate (the process of settlement) it becomes a matter of public record. That includes the terms of any trust under the will.

Right about now you may be wondering, "When should a living trust be used, and when a testamentary?" The answer is, "It depends." It depends upon purpose, duration required, perhaps amount involved, terms of distribution, and other factors.

Here is an example of a situation in which there would have been little point in establishing a living trust when a testamentary trust would accomplish the purpose.

A relatively young woman had become widowed. She had a son with seven years of school remaining. Her estate was a very modest one, and her concern was that her son be taken care of until he graduated, first as to living expenses, and second as to costs of education if possible.

A trust under the will was used. The amount to go into trust in event of the mother's death would not be large. It would gradually be diminished by payment for bills for the son. A trust would not be called for after the boy had finished school as he would then be of age, and his mother was willing that he should have outright any remaining funds.

In a number of the illustrative cases which follow you will be able to see why some called for living trusts, and some for testamentary trusts. It is better to rely upon the advices of competent counsel in the matter of choice rather than to choose arbitrarily for yourself.

Other Personal Trusts

There are other less frequently used trust forms: trusts for special purposes, temporary trusts, and "short term" trusts. The last mentioned is an income tax saving device of practical use only to persons in fairly high income tax brackets.

Since all of these are unlikely to be of general interest, and since any one of them should be understood thoroughly before entering into its establishment, and since all require construction and drafting by a competent attorney, we will not go into details.

Just so it is not thought to have been overlooked, we will mention a trust form at the other end of the spectrum from the short-term trust.

This is the very simple type of trust used in such instances as the establishment of a savings account for a child recorded as being "In trust for ————." If you contemplate creating "in trust for" ownership for a minor, do be certain to find out from the person with whom you are working what the legal and tax implications are.

Another form of trust is widely used, and is of considerable importance to those who are married. It is known as the "marital deduction" trust. Since it is involved with estate settlement and estate taxes we will treat it in the next chapter which has to do with wills and estate matter.

Why a Trust?

Who needs a trust? Why? The best way to answer these questions is by answering another: what purpose can trusts serve? Recognizing the purposes that can be served, and matching them against your own objectives you can ascertain fairly easily whether or not a trust can be useful in your plans. Here are some of the purposes served by trusts along with brief descriptions of actual cases in point.

1. FINANCIAL PROTECTION AND CARE. This usually applies to dependents or loved ones who by reason of age, disability, disposition, or other reasons lack the ability or desire to apply proper attention and controls to financial matters. This includes minors and incompetents, but not exclusively so. It may even include the settlor who does not like handling investments and money matters, and does not want to be concerned with them, or feels the need for someone to handle her affairs in the event of emergency.

Mrs. R., a widow, has an adult daughter who is able to work at a very simple job, but who cannot begin to cope with life's problems of financial cares, taxes, or much else beyond basic, daily personal matters. Mrs. R. has a life insurance trust into which not only her life insurance will be paid, but all the remainder of her property except for a couple of small direct bequests. Her attorney thought that the advantages of a life insurance trust made it more desirable than a testamentary trust for her.

Another case is that of an elderly retired professional person who just "got tired of all the bills and checks and taxes and forms." In this case the protection was needed personally so that bills would not be overlooked or tax payments missed. A living trust was just the answer. The trustee took over all the financial responsibilities.

A different situation exists with another

friend. She admits quite frankly: "It's good my husband left things in trust for me. I like to spend money and not worry about trying to take care of it. This way I get along just fine."

2. INVESTMENT MANAGEMENT. This means the professional handling and care of investments before or after death.

Investment management undoubtedly was in the mind of the husband of the woman in the story just told. That is an after-death case.

A living trust solved the problem in a before-death case. There is the case of a lady whose two brothers had taken care of her financial affairs for her for years. Finally for very good reasons, they decided they should no longer do it. Their sister's background includes almost nothing of a financial nature beyond keeping her check book. She has put her investments into a living trust. The trustee will manage the portfolio for her.

3. CONTROL OF EXPENDITURES. Here again this may be a before-death or an after-death purpose.

If you leave me $20,000 outright under your will, and express the wish that I use it only to educate Joe or Nancy, or that I keep it to do thus and so eventually, it may not work out that way. I may decide to have some fun at the racetrack with it, and that's that.

But if you want control by someone after you are gone, you can get it by having that $20,000 as part of a trust.

Two daughters were beneficiaries under a trust, their parents being deceased. I guess daddy knew his daughters because they certainly came up with some real gems of requests for money from the trustee. The trustee just kept saying "no," but reminding them that for medical bills, for college bills if they would return to college, for necessities, the money would be forthcoming promptly—but not for some of the purposes they had dreamed up. I am sure that is exactly what their father would have wanted the trustee to say. The trust is the one way to assure discretionary control out in the future.

4. FLEXIBILITY. This is somewhat like "3" although the control may be relinquished to the beneficiary by a right of withdrawal. Many trusts have withdrawal provisions either at will or under certain circumstances.

5. INCOME TO SOME, CASH TO OTHERS. A common provision of trusts is to provide that a beneficiary will receive income up to a certain age, or ages, and then cash. This means that older beneficiaries may receive cash while younger ones are still receiving income.

I know of one case in which there are two sons. Son One is a successful professional man.

Son Two is an artist who has had little success, and who knows little and cares less about money. Under the mother's will son One will receive cash. Son Two will have income from a trust with power in the trustee to pay out principal for medical or other emergencies.

6. CHARITABLE OBJECTIVES. A recent case will probably serve to explain better than lengthy description. Here are the facts.

Unmarried woman. Mother living, comfortably fixed financially, but not wealthy. Daughter wants to be assured that if she dies there will be funds available for mother if mother's own funds are exhausted. Daughter really wants her money to go to a college for music scholarships.

Answer. Testamentary trust was executed. It provides for daughter's estate to go into trust. If mother lives she becomes income beneficiary for her life, with rights in trustee to invade the principal of the trust for medical or other necessities for her benefit. If mother is not living at daughter's death, or when she dies subsequently, trust continues with income going to the college for the prescribed scholarship purposes.

Another woman established a trust with the income retained for herself during life, and then at her death the entire amount of the trust fund goes to a college.

Still another woman has done the same with the remainder at her death being divided 10 percent to a few relatives and 90 percent to a hospital.

To make certain of the best tax advantages it is important that charitable trusts be drafted very carefully. The Tax Reform Act of 1969 effected major changes in requirements, so it is not safe to be guided by the way daddy, or auntie, or someone you heard about arranged a charitable trust many years ago.

Other Related Services

Custodial accounts. I have a friend who was a career officer in the army. Stationed here and there around the world, he needed a home base for his securities. He arranged for a custodial account with a trust company. It held his securities, and did as he directed with interest and dividends. Purchases and sales were made only at my friend's direction. This made the account a "directed" one. Had he authorized the trust company to buy and sell without orders from him it would have been a "nondirected" or discretionary custodial account.

Investment management services—called by a variety of names—are offered by numerous trust companies under a variety of arrangements.

Guardianship. Minors without parents, and others who are "incompetent" in the sense of being unable to perform acts of legal effect, need guardians to act for them.

A guardianship may be only that of the person. "Susie, brush your teeth." "Joe, we are going to the store now. You need some new shirts." "You kids get ready for school."

The guardianship of property may be the responsibility of someone else, or of an institution, perhaps a trust company.

Or the same person may be total guardian.

Often a trust is provided to take care of the property aspects, the trustee making disbursements to the guardian of the person so that food, clothing and other needs are paid for.

Courts are very jealous of the rights of minors and other legal incompetents. They quite properly want accurate accounting and handling of funds. For this reason, as well as that of the direct benefit of the minor, it is important to weigh the attributes and abilities of anyone you are thinking of nominating as guardian. (The court will make the final determination.)

Suitability of a trust depends upon many factors including how much is involved and how long would a guardianship probably exist. A trust would seem to make little sense for a small estate which would pass to a minor who is already within a year of attaining majority.

Pension trusts, and others. Though not personal trusts, pension trusts and profit-sharing trusts are numerous. These are employee-benefit trusts. They are paid for in whole or in part by the employer for the ultimate benefit of employees.

If you are employed by a company which has a pension or profit-sharing trust you should make sure that you become informed by reading the descriptive material, or by discussion with the appropriate person in your company. It will be very much worth your while. Re-read the story at the end of the section Information Please in Chapter One.

HR 10 (Keogh) Plans. These plans provide an opportunity for self-employed persons to set aside money for retirement on a tax deductible basis. They may be invested in various ways such as life insurance, mutual funds, and other securities including government obligations. Your banker, insurance adviser, savings and loan officer, or investment adviser can provide you with details including requirements and restrictions of eligibility and of acceptable provisions of the trust.

Individual Retirement Accounts. A self-employed person or a person not covered by a pension, profit-sharing, or Keogh plan is eligible to establish one of these accounts. A trustee or custodian must be used. Savings accounts, "C.D.'s," savings certificates, special government retirement bonds, certain restricted endowment insurance contracts, and retirement annuities are included on the list of approved investments for "IRA's."

As in the case of the Keogh plans, there are numerous restrictions and requirements for a plan to meet qualifications for tax deductibility of contributions. Your advisers can guide you.

Fees

Anyone contemplating the use of trust services is likely to wonder about fees involved. Normally this concern should not be of consequence. If the need for the trust is marginal and the amount to be put into the trust is small, then the matter of a minimum fee may have some bearing since the need is not critical. Usually, however, the fee should not be the determining factor. (Once again: "Objectives.")

This raises two questions. How small is too small? Or to put it another way, what should one consider to be a minimum practical amount to establish a trust?

There is no universal criterion. One institution with excellent trust services considers $40,000 to be a practical minimum, because the minimum fee would consume what might well be considered too large a part of the earnings of a smaller trust. Yet this institution has many smaller trusts because a trust was the only answer to some particular problems. The institution does not make a profit on such accounts even after a minimum fee, but it is satisfied to render service because that service provides the only real solution for the customer.

I have heard officers of trust companies located in large cities say that they think a proper minimum is $100,000 or more. But questioning develops the answer that they really do not hold to that if circumstances dictate otherwise.

The second question asked is, "What are the fees?" In the great majority of cases the answer is, "Reasonable." If that sounds like a generalization, that is exactly what it is.

I had occasion a few years ago to make fee comparisons of four sizeable trust institutions serving the same moderately-large area of rural and urban population. The formulae varied. There were some differences in what type of charge was made for particular kinds of trusts. But a person would have had to be able to predict the future duration of the trust, the investment results, and other unknowns to be able to say that one fee schedule was more attractive than another.

After all, trust institutions must be competitive, so the answer really is "Reasonable." Just ask. Fee schedules are not top-secret documents.

Taxes

The matter of taxation of personal trusts should not be of concern to most persons who are considering the use of a trust.

That is not to say that trust taxation is not a world

of its own, which is often complicated. But that is the concern and responsibility of the trustee. Trust officers often have to dig into the tax books, but handling the reports and tax payments is one of the jobs a trustee is paid to do.

A simplified statement for purposes of our general consideration is: income which is passed on by the trust to the beneficiary is taxed to the beneficiary, not to the trust.

As in the case of fees, taxes should not be thought of as a factor except in unusual cases.

Some Pitfalls

1. Should you find a trust useful in your situation, do keep in mind that it should be reviewed as your objectives (there is that word again!) change and as circumstances alter.

2. There is a minimum size at which a trust ceases to be practical. This varies with a particular institution's fee schedule, with the purpose for which trust income is to be put, and with the rate at which principal is to be disbursed. A trust officer can advise you.

3. Non-income producing property ordinarily does not make a good trust asset. It produces no income, and often is a drain on other trust income, such as taxes which have to be paid on undeveloped real estate.

There are valid exceptions, but the point is worth remembering.

4. If property is to go into a trust, be certain it gets there. I have seen more than one life insurance trust which called for the proceeds of certain policies to be paid to the trust. Then when I looked at the policies I have found that no change of beneficiary to the trust had been effected.

5. Trusts need to be personalized. Trusts are legal instruments. It is not a good idea to copy a trust designed for someone else. Have your own properly drafted by your attorney.

6. Choose your trustee wisely. Corporate trustees do not die; individual trustees do. Corporate trustees do not become disabled, nor do they retire or move away.

There are instances in which a personal trustee might be satisfactory, such as for a trust for a family member designed only to be in effect for a year or so, or possibly for a "short-term" trust. If a personal trustee is to be used, that person should be competent to handle the requirements for investing, reporting, filing proper tax returns, and generally administering the trust. Being a good, honest person is not always enough for the job.

*   *   *   *   *

Most trust officers will be glad to talk with you at

any reasonable length to answer questions, or explain in detail some of the subject matter covered in this chapter. Trust institutions do not want dissatisfied customers. If a trust really does not fit your circumstances you will almost surely be told so. Your attorney, too, can give you the benefit of his experience and thoughts on how, or if, a trust would accomplish your objectives.

Questions on Chapter Seven

1. What is the purpose of a trust? Who are the usual parties to a trust?

2. What is a living trust?

3. What is a life insurance trust?

4. What is a testamentary trust?

5. What are four or five reasons why people create trusts?

6. What is a Keogh or HR 10 plan?

7. What is an Individual Retirement Account (IRA)?

8. What are some common pitfalls in trust considerations and in actions which might or might not be taken?

VIII

The Will and the Way

Who needs a will—Why—First considerations of bequests and executor—Other important considerations for a will—Wills and trusts— How they work together—Examples—Marital deduction

Post Mortem

Perhaps the question most frequently asked of us who lecture or conduct seminars on estate planning subjects is, "Why should I have a will?" Then this is followed by one of these statements.

1. "I am not married, so everything would go to my mother (or father, or brothers and sisters) anyway."

or

2. "I own everything jointly with my husband (or sister or mother) so it would all go to the survivor without a will."

or

3. "I am all alone, and I don't really care what happens to my estate after I am gone."

In order to dispose of the question, and the usual follow-up statements, let us take them one by one.

1. Maybe what is said will happen. Maybe not. It depends on your state's intestacy law.

   But look what can happen. Take the case of assuming that everything will be divided among brothers and sisters. Suppose your sister dies before you do, and she leaves children. I have before me a summary of one state's law on that. The sister's children would take her share. Perhaps you would want that, or perhaps not. It shows what can happen.

   But take the case of assuming that all would go to your surviving mother. Suppose she dies, and thereafter you just do not get around to having a will executed. Then what? Even if you have brothers or sisters, would you want total and equal division to be made, or would you want certain property to go to particular ones?

2. "My husband and I (or my mother or sister and I) own everything jointly." "Everything?" Oh, come now. Does the husband jointly own the wife's diamonds, fur, heirlooms from her side of the family, perhaps the car she drives, or a savings account in her name? Does the wife own jointly with the husband his several hun-

dred dollars worth of tools, his gun collection, the car registered in his name, the boat? And what of pension fund rights of either spouse?

All right, if you insist that everything is jointly held, then how about this? Husband and wife are in a common accident. He dies at once. The joint property becomes hers. She lingers, and dies a month or so later before recovering, and certainly before getting around to thinking through the terms of a will and having one prepared. She then dies intestate—certainly not what either spouse wanted or anticipated.

People do not always die in the order prescribed by either reason or mortality tables.

Furthermore, it is likely that your state has a statute covering the presumption to be made if a common disaster strikes a married couple in such way as to make it impossible to determine who dies first. Absent instructions in the will as to what shall be the presumption, or in the case of intestacy the statute prevails.

In some states, as an example, the presumption for estate purposes is that each survived the other. This often results in a situation which is the least desirable from both a tax and distribution standpoint. The legislators are not to be faulted. The same could be said of any presumptive statute. The solution is a properly drafted will.

This all adds to the importance of a will for

each spouse, joint property holdings notwith-standing.

In the case of property held jointly by persons other than husband and wife there can be all sorts of complications, not the least of which is the matter of taxation. A portion of the next chapter will be devoted to the subject of joint property and some important considerations to be weighed before creating joint tenancies.

3. I find it very difficult to believe that, despite what they may say, people who are all alone do not really care what happens to what they have accumulated over the years.

I know one woman who has no children by either her first or second marriage. The couple of distant relatives there are have never been close to her or she to them. She could say, "I don't care," but she has provided nominal amounts to them, a couple of bequests to friends, and all else to charity.

Another friend of mine, a widower, with no children has two nephews, distant both in terms of geography and in terms of any endearment. Under his state's intestacy laws these two would "take."

I do not know that he really has decided to whom he wants to leave his rather considerable estate. "I guess I'll leave it to them," he says. But if he does, he will do it by design, not by inaction.

There is one more very good reason for making a will. It is the one way you can determine who is to wind up your affairs, who really will stand in your stead and represent you after you are gone. Without the will your estate will be settled by an administrator appointed by the court. Whether that be a person or an institutional administrator the court's selection would almost surely be reliable enough, but that does not mean that it would have been the choice you would have made. The only way to be sure is to name your own executor, and if you name a person rather than an institution you would do well to name a contingent executor, too. (More of that thought subsequently.)

Anyone interested enough in the subject matter of this book to read it needs a will. Even those women—and men—who insist that their estates are too small to make a will worthwhile, may be very wrong. In the first place, the valuation placed on any individual's estate may be higher than expected, but there is another reason.

Many states have a Small Estates Statute (by whatever name) which provides that an estate of less than a certain value, perhaps $5,000, may be settled by appropriate heirs without the usual probate process.

Interestingly, one of my attorney friends who does a considerable amount of probate work tells me that, based upon his experience, he would prefer to settle one of these small estates under a well-drawn, simple will. He says it "works out as easily or better" than under the special act for small estates.

You may recall Huck from Chapter Three. I am sure that Huck had no will any more than he would have had insurance. True enough he probably needed no will, nor would anyone like him. But how many Hucks are there around these days?

First Considerations

Here comes that same old first step again: establish objectives. There is little point in talking with your attorney, or a trust officer, or your insurance adviser until you have thought through some *general* wishes and aims. These advisers cannot tell you what you want to do in terms of who is to get what, or in some cases when and under what terms they are to get it. Objectives come first. In most of the decisions about your estate distribution it is a matter not of right vs. wrong, but of your preferences. Those are personal decisions.

When it comes to how best to accomplish what you want—tax planning, insurance planning, trust planning, and that sort of thing—good advisers are essential. Basic choices, however, are yours to make.

Here are a few matters you may want to consider.

As you begin to think about matters of distribution, bear in mind that it is impossible for you to know the exact amount of what your distributable estate will be. There will be last expenses, unpaid obligations even if only current bills, taxes, fees, court costs, etc. Furthermore values of stocks, bonds, real estate, antiques all vary from time to time. In this initial stage of thinking about what distribution you want it is best to think in approximations.

The one phase of initial thinking in which *specifics* are to be considered is that of bequests of certain items of VALUABLE property to certain people.

If you want a niece to have your piano, your brother to have your cottage by the lake, your sister to have your automobile and your diamond ring, then make some notes accordingly. No adviser can decide those choices for you. They are purely personal. Sometimes the decisions are not easy. Recently, after I had urged one woman to make her list of specific items of bequest, I found that it took her two or three weeks, but when she had finished she was pleased with her decisions. Moreover, she had not taken the time of her attorney (time for which she would have been paying) while she sat there to "think out loud" about it.

Perhaps you noticed in the above paragraph the description used was "VALUABLE property." The implication is that a list of specific bequests not include items of trivial value or of purely sentimental worth. ("The silver earrings I brought back from Taxco.") I know of one instance of a woman who left a vine "with its roots" to a friend!

I recall one woman who had about ten of these unusual bequests in her will, which was then perhaps 15 years-old. She was in her eighties. Several of the people whom she had named were deceased. I am not sure that all the items were still among her effects. Her attorney and I pleaded with her to change the will. She never did, and she died a few months later. The result was that her executor was left with the moral and legal obligation of trying to locate the objects and the legatees if they were still alive.

I had a beloved and wise professor who said, "Reminiscences are usually more interesting to the one doing the reminiscing than to the listeners." The same is to be said of sentimental gifts and recipients. The latter usually feel much less sentimental attachments than do the original owners.

So what disposition does one make of small, not valuable articles? Three answers:

1. Make gifts during lifetime. This affords the pleasure of giving and the certainty of knowing that the person you wish to have the object really gets it before it is mislaid, lost or broken.

2. If there are to be only a couple of recipients have a clause in the will which says "as they may amicably agree." If agreement cannot be reached then the executor can sell the property and put the cash in the estate.

3. Have a memo accompanying the will setting

forth your list. It may or may not be referred to
in the will.*

It is best to follow your own attorney's advice, as
he likely would be the one concerned with any subsequent arguments which might arise.

I have seen all three methods used by competent attorneys, and I have never seen any of the three result
in litigation. Please keep in mind that we are considering here only articles of no great value. The list
idea should not even be considered for valuable
property.

———————

Another early consideration to be made is this
question. "Do I have any contingent bequests to
make?" An example: "I want my mother to have
such and such property or income if she is alive."
What if she is not? Then what about that property,
or possibly that income? Who is to have it?"

This question may go a step further with the
question, "Is the next person to get it outright, or is

———————

* Some attorneys think suggestion "2" can lead to arguments.
Some attorneys do not like "3," the idea of a list, or if a list the
idea of the reference on the grounds that arguments may arise as to
whether the list thereby really becomes testamentary. Some prefer
no reference but a clause in the will allowing distribution "in
kind" (property, not cash only) so that the executor can distribute
as per the terms of the memo.

there to be some deferral predicated upon time, or the person's age, or the happening of some event such as attending college?''

Another thought for this preliminary pondering is: "Do I wish to make a bequest to a charitable institution, educational institution, hospital, or other qualified institution?"

Charitable bequests are deductible for tax purposes. There are even ways of leaving income to living person/s with the principal ultimately going to the charitable institution. This is a somewhat complex business which demands competent legal attention to the terms, but it can be done.

The question is: "Am I interested in making some bequest/s for charitable purposes?" If "yes," then your adviser can guide you from there.

Still another important consideration is that of who the executor is to be. ("Executrix" if a woman. For simplicity we will use "executor.")

Being an executor is not an easy job. It carries responsibilities and liabilities for failure to perform properly. In all but the smallest and simplest estates the task calls for someone who not only knows what needs to be done, but how to do it, or at least where to go to find out how to do it. There is everything from probating the will, to advertising for the attention of creditors, to meeting tax deadlines, to being responsible for property, and for proper distribution.

Here is an example of that last point. I know one executor who discovered on a visit to the deceased's home that some of the family members had decided to help themselves to a valuable gun collection, and divide it among themselves. The executor had the unpleasant job of retrieving all of the guns. This shows the sort of thing that can happen.

A family member, even if competent, may not be the best executor. I have known more than one person who refused to name a family member. There are two good reasons. (1) Conflict of interest is almost certain to arise if the situation involves brothers, sisters or possibly children. (2) Even with the best of intentions and correct actions, the executor who is a family member is likely to evoke criticism, hard feelings, and perhaps jealousy.

Your attorney may want to be your executor, but many law firms have a definite rule that their members may not accept executorships. If you do decide to name your attorney and he agrees to it, keep in mind that he may be deceased, disabled, retired, or living in another part of the country when you die. Insist upon a contingent executor being named.

Trust institutions should be considered. People die. Corporations do not. Professionals administer wills and trusts in trust institutions. They know the taxes, practices, laws and regulations.

All estates do not need corporate executors. Many estates should use them, probably many more than do.

Other Considerations

1. Professional preparation. Another frequent question to come up in seminars is, "Can't I write my own will since I don't have much of an estate?" Answer: "Yes, you can, but don't."

   No doubt you have read some newsy case of the fellow who wrote a will on an old brown bag, and it was found to be valid. But you do not read of the cases such as one I encountered when finally getting a client to the attorney's office. Proudly he displayed his homemade will. The attorney took one look and said, "I have news for you. This wouldn't stand up for five minutes in court." Nor have you read of another case I know of which has been bouncing around in various courts for several years, because no one knows yet what the testator meant by certain sections of his self-drawn will.

   Whatever it costs to have your will drawn in your community, it is such a small part of your estate it is worth the fee to be sure. Come to think of it, the last case on which I consulted resulted in an attorney's fee which was a small fraction of one-percent of the estate value. Attorneys do not relate fees to a percentage of the estate; more and more they charge on a time basis. The illustration merely indicates the relative relationship. It pays in the matter of a will to be certain that you are right. You will not be around to say, "That is not what I meant to do at all."

2. Location. Question: "Where shall I keep my will?" Answer: "In a safe place." Safe deposit box. (See next chapter.) Fireproof vault or safe. If a corporate executor or trustee is named, the institution probably will keep the documents for you without charge.

If your will is burned, stolen, destroyed, or lost, make it Priority One for replacement.

3. Who should know? As to what it says —probably no one except you, your attorney, and possibly your executor. You might change your mind and then you will not be embarrassed to change the provisions. As to where it is—two or three people should know so it can be located quickly. As to copies—your attorney will keep one; you may want to keep a copy for reference without having to go to the bank or to an office vault. If a trust company is executor or trustee it should have either the original or a copy.

4. Instructions for funeral or burial. Not in a will, please. It is not unusual for a will to be left untouched for a couple of days or more following testator's death. What else can be the case if death occurs Friday evening or Saturday, and

the bank does not reopen until Monday, and the will is in your safe deposit box?

It is far better to leave the instructions, sealed if you like, with someone (better yet, two people) who will be among the first to know: close relative, friend, rabbi, priest, or minister, neighbor, to suggest a few possibilities.

5. Bequests in fractions. It has been said above that one really cannot know exactly what there will be left to distribute after bills, fees, taxes, etc.

For this reason it is often wise to make disposition of the residual estate (what is left for distribution after specific bequests) in fractional amounts.

Here is a good example of one career woman's estate plan. The will provided for payment of bills and taxes, for certain bequests of particular items (mostly of family heirlooms), and then $\frac{1}{6}$ of the residual to each of four nephews and nieces, and the remaining $\frac{1}{3}$ divided among five other people. It worked out very smoothly.

6. Changes. Perhaps you already have a will. Good. But the best of wills need reviewing at least every two years. They may not require changing, but again they may. People die. We become disappointed or disillusioned with friends or relatives or charities. Circumstances

change. A sister marries. A brother becomes disabled. We sell property. We buy property. Changes!

7. Witnesses. It is desirable that persons chosen to witness a will be ones who are likely to be available at the time of death of the testator. This means that it is good practice to select younger people who have some likelihood of continuing to live in the vicinity.

One attorney friend urged me to include that statement because of his experiences in probating wills which out-of-town or deceased persons had witnessed. Not that failure of the will is likely, but difficulty and delays can result.

Taking a good look at what a will provides is well worth the doing periodically. Sometimes we find we have forgotten what we did provide for.

There are two avenues open to you if you wish to make some changes in your will.

A *codicil* is an amendment to a will. In most states it requires the same formality of dating and witnessing along with signature as does a will. It is not unusual for a will to have more than one codicil. Right now mine has two.

If the change you want to make is not lengthy, and if it does not involve a number of sections of the will your attorney will probably recommend using a codicil to effect the change/s.

If, however, the changes are numerous, and especially if they involve different sections of the will, he will probably advise the second course: rewriting the will.

Either way is equally effective. It is just a question of which is the more simple way to handle the change.

Wills and Trustees

Having read the chapter on trusts, and having considered some of the possible objectives you might have for your own estate plans, you are now in a position to appreciate how wills and trust often work together.

The *testamentary* trust, you will recall, is a trust under a will.

The *living trust* is in existence at the time of death and was probably written to provide for acceptance of property from the estate, or from other sources.

Examples will very likely be more helpful than lengthy technical expositions of the uses.

Case A. Retired professional woman. Two brothers. One alert and able to handle his affairs, but does not think his handling affairs for other brother a good idea. Other brother not well, not very adept with financial matters.

Solution: Ms. X, after a few specific bequests in her will, leaves the one brother one-half the residue outright. The other half goes into a testamentary trust with income to the second brother with power in the trustee to invade the principal for medical or other necessary purposes.

Case B. Widowed grandmother. Sufficiently well off that she can give away funds. Made gifts (see next chapter about gifts and gift taxes) to an irrevocable trust with income to grandchildren until a certain time and then cash.

This removes the money from her estate and means that she can eliminate the grandchildren under her will.

She herself is receiving income from trusts under her late husband's estate.

Case C. Grandmother. Son highly successful; says he does not want anything from her estate. She does not like daughter-in-law.

Solution: Trust, either living or testamentary, to provide at grandmother's death for income for grandchildren's benefit until some reasonably mature ages, then distribution to them.

The problem is that grandmother is a great procrastinator, and she has done nothing to implement the solution. I have a feeling that she never will get around to doing so. There are two words to describe procrastination on the part of anyone involved with any part of estate planning: *no good*.

Incidentally, this example is equally appropriate if brothers, sisters, nephews or nieces were involved instead of children and grandchildren.

Case D and E. Very similar cases. These two women have dependent mothers in ailing conditions. In each case daughter wants to assure needed income for mother. Each woman has testamentary trust providing income for mother with ultimate distribution to others at mother's death, or immediately if mother has predeceased daughter.

A review of the last chapter having to do with trusts, and what they can accomplish in appropriate cases, might prove helpful if you conceptualize those in which a trust and your will together may solve a particular problem which you have. If you think this is even a possibility, it would be a good idea to talk it over with your advisers.

Case F. The marital deduction trust. There are thousands of these in use. Their importance deserves separate treatment.

The Marital Deduction

If you are not married, or if you presently have no concern of any kind in the settlement or planning of an estate of a married couple you may find little of interest in this last section of the chapter. It covers a subject of great importance for married persons, especially from a tax standpoint.

Its application to gifts will be touched upon in the next chapter. Here we are concerned with the use of the marital deduction in the final estate plans. Proper steps taken by a married couple can result in minimizing the total tax impact on the estate.

The Tax Reform Act of 1976 made a multitude of far-reaching changes in the Estate and Gift Tax laws. Among these is a whole set of new rules as to what joint property is includable in the estate of a decedent.

It should be noted that for Federal Estate Tax purposes "estate" includes life insurance owned by a decedent and often part or all of the joint property in which the decedent had an interest.

The proper interplay of these forms of property as they are utilized within the framework of the marital deduction is extremely important.

If you are thinking that the subject is complex and filled with technicalities, you are so right. For that reason, it must be clearly and strongly stated here that what follows is no more than superficial treatment of the subject, enough to describe what it is and how it works. A basic understanding may be helpful in exploring advantages and avoiding mistakes.

Competent professional work is required for any application of the principles.

How It Works

The marital deduction is allowed to married persons (either spouse) for Federal Estate and Gift Tax purposes. (For Gift Tax implications, please see next chapter.) In essence, it provides that to the extent property is left to the control* of the surviving spouse:

1. The first $250,000 passes tax free to that surviving spouse,

or

2. If *one-half* the estate is in excess of $250,000 then that amount passes tax-free to the surviving spouse.

The advantage of the marital deduction, through its workings, comes in this fashion. The deceased spouse has the tax benefit in his or her estate. More than that, even though the surviving spouse will have no marital deduction except in the case of remarriage, he or she may have used some of the inherited estate so that part will not be taxable at the death of the surviving spouse. Furthermore, the surviving spouse has his or her own tax *credits* toward federal taxes (see next chapter) at the time of his or her subsequent death, even if there has been no remarriage, and hence no new marital deduction.

---

* The word "control" is used for ease of understanding. It obviously includes outright bequests, but it also includes trusts which grand certain powers to the surviving spouse.

To married taxpayers the advantages are considerable.

If you live in a state with COMMUNITY PROPERTY laws by all means consult counsel as to how the above applies in your state.

One common type of arrangement to secure maximum benefits of the marital deduction is the use of a trust or two trusts which will effect the tax savings, and also provide the desired distribution at the death of the survivor. The accompanying diagram and explanation shows how this plan works.

After you have studied the diagram for just a few minutes you will have grasped the general idea, even if you previously had no knowledge of the marital deduction or its operation. The simplification used in the diagram and its explanation does not imply an equivalent simplification in the preparation or terms of the documents required to achieve the desired results.

Notes about the diagram:

1. Side A is known as the "qualifying" side. Property "qualifies" if it meets the minimum requirement that the surviving spouse has at least the right to appoint the person/s to whom such property is to pass at his/her death.

2. Joint property under tenancy by entirety, or with right of survivorship is "qualifying" property.

3. Life insurance proceeds "qualify" if they meet at least the minimum requirements, as in "1" above.

4. A side is not taxed at this death, but whatever remains of it at surviving spouse's death will be part of his/her estate, and subject to taxes and credits at that time. B side is taxable at the first death.

5. An estate need not use the maximum amounts permitted for qualification. Often there are reasons not to do so.

The Marital Deduction

Gross Estate

less

Debts and Expenses

leaves

Adjusted Gross Estate

Qualifying	Non-qualifying
A	**B**
Side under spouse's control: non-taxable up to $250,000, or up to ½ the estate if ½ is in excess of $250,000	Taxable side:
	Bequests to other than spouse
	Bequests to spouse in excess of ½ estate if ½ estate is more than $250,000.
Includes outright bequests to spouse, and/or	"B" trust described below, and then to:
"A" trust described below. If trust used then to:	

ultimate beneficiaries
or remaindermen

ultimate beneficiaries
or remaindermen

(A) This side represents either a trust with broad powers to the surviving spouse, or outright bequest. If trust is used the remaining principal may be distributed as directed after death of the surviving spouse.

(B) This side represents a trust with income to the surviving spouse for life (usually) then distribution or continuation of trust as directed. It also includes bequests to others.

It is not always advisable to use the maximum marital deduction. To do so may force the surviving spouse's estate into an unfavorable tax position. There are other possible reasons, too. Be sure to provide your adviser, and especially your attorney with all pertinent facts.

For three decades the marital deduction has been available and widely used. Those who have availed themselves of it have saved tax dollars for their own estates or for those of their surviving spouses. Perhaps even more importantly, in most cases they have provided a smooth transition for the passing of property to loved ones.

Now that the 1976 Tax Reform Act has liberalized the provisions of the marital deduction it has become even more important in estate plans than before.

* * * * *

Whether your needs are for those of a simple will or for a not-so-simple marital deduction trust they should be attended to, and then reviewed, periodically. After you are gone it is too, too late.

Questions on Chapter Eight

1. What are the main reasons that most people should have wills?

2. What are some of the subjects one might well think about before consulting any professional advisers?

3. How can distribution of small, not valuable items be made?

4. Can you name at least five considerations other than the initial ones you named in answer to question 2?

5. What is a codicil and when is it likely to be used?

6. Can you give some examples—not necessarily those provided in this chapter—of how wills and trusts can work together in sound estate plans?

7. Could you explain to a friend the basic principles of the marital deduction?

8. Do you have an up-to-date will?

IX

—and a Number of Other Matters

Safe Deposit—Power of Attorney—Gifts—
Reasons for care in making gifts—Joint
Property—Starting a Business—Taxes—Final
Pot Pourri.

Handle with Care

The caption does not imply danger, per se, but rather the hazard of improper usage. The finest of kitchen cutlery can cut fingers as well as trim steaks.

The subject matter of this chapter has to do with proper uses and precautions for safety (in a financial sense) when using certain financial and estate "tools," and services.

The order of treatment does not imply order of importance, for the reason that one subject which may be of vital import to one person will never be contemplated by another.

Safe-Deposit Boxes

The purpose and availability of safe-deposit boxes are too well-known to call for explanation. Charges are modest and the safekeeping performance record of institutions offering safe-deposit services is excellent.

Some papers should be retained in a safe-deposit box: birth certificates, marriage certificates, military papers of importance, stock certificates, bonds, deeds and for many people their wills, to mention a few. Most of these could be replaced, but it would take time and might be somewhat expensive, depending upon circumstances.

There is little point in keeping insurance policies in a safe-deposit box. In the first place, reference to the policies is probably more frequent than to many other documents. That is not possible of an evening or a weekend when the institution where the policies are kept is closed.

More than that, however, insurance policies are not negotiable. If a life insurance policy is lost or stolen the finder or thief cannot take it to a bank and cash it.

If the policies are burned or otherwise destroyed, either certificates representing them, or duplicate policies can be issued. Keeping a list of companies and policy numbers in the safe-deposit box is a good idea, but practicality dictates against keeping the policies there even if there is adequate space for them.

Papers which have long since outlived any usefulness should be destroyed. Left in a safe-deposit box, your executor will think that they must be important for some reason. Much needless querying and searching may result.

One question which seems to have more answers based on rumors than on facts is that of, "What is permitted regarding access to a box which is jointly held when one of the joint holders dies?"

The correct answer to the question depends upon the law of the state where the box is located. "Sealing" is commonly done under specified circumstances. That simply means no access to the box is allowed until properly authorized persons are on hand to make sure an inventory is made, or to witness that only a will is removed. After all, the taxing authorities do not want anyone to abscond with the crown jewels that had been stashed away in the box.

One state directs sealing at the death of either co-holding spouse, although the survivor may have access a single time to procure the will. Another state allows complete access to the surviving spouse.

Non-spouse joint holders in each of these states find the box sealed at the death of either.

Unsealing will take place after inventory of contents in the box.

People tend to think of the joint holding arrangement as a convenience. Often it is, but it has the access-at-death problem to whatever extent that is a problem in your state.

In the case of spouses, there are advantages to having separate boxes. For example, the original of my will is in my wife's safe-deposit box, and the original of hers is in mine. Our boxes are in separate names.

Another possibility for access is through the use of a power of attorney. Since that is our next subject, its uses and some examples will be covered in the following paragraphs.

Power of Attorney

The power of attorney is an authority given in writing by the grantor to another person, who may then act for the one who gave the authority to do so. The power may be *limited* or it may be *general*.

The *limited power* is typified by that used in connection with services of financial institutions.

My wife had an elderly aunt who was having difficulty in walking any great distance. In addition to that her eyesight was failing. For these reasons she wanted me to take care of her banking, pay her bills by checks on her account, effect any desired transfers from her checking account to her savings account and vice versa, etc.

Furthermore she wanted me to have access to her safe-deposit box—not only to put in or take out valuable articles—but even more than that to have access to her securities. If we decided to sell any, or, as did happen in one instance, the need arose to get a particular stock certificate for some special reason, we could get what we needed.

A limited power of attorney enabled me to take care of these matters for her. Banking and savings and loan institutions make available to their customers the proper forms for granting a limited power of attorney to provide the necessary legal authority for banking and safe-deposit purposes.

The *general power* is not restricted as is a limited power. It is just what it says: general.

A good example of the proper usage of the general power is provided by its widespread use by the military, especially during, but certainly not restricted to, times of war.

Women and men of the military services may be sent anywhere at any time for prolonged durations. They need someone back home with power to act for them. This is particularly so in situations with deadlines for action. Even in routine situations reasonably prompt action is usually desirable. If someone back home can act under a general power, how much better it is than to suffer delays, crosses in the mail, missed deadlines for action, and possibly missed opportunities for buying, selling, conversions, or exchanges.

The need is not limited to those in the military, or away for long periods, or even those confined by some disability.

With all of the above reasons for the usage of the power of attorney, you may be wondering why the subject falls in a chapter captioned "Handle with Care."

The reasons are twofold. One is from the standpoint of the grantor, and one from the standpoint of the one acting under the power.

A story in which I was a participant just two or three years ago will illustrate both sides.

An elderly woman, like my wife's aunt in the story above, was having difficulty in physical movement and severe eye failure.

Her attorney and I were working with her on some other matters when she volunteered the information that she thought advantage was being taken of her. A much younger woman was handling her banking and paying her bills. The client did not think that everything was in order, and indeed, that there may have been some misappropriation of funds.

We asked to see what records and reports she had. She produced them, and we made a quick review. It did appear that not everything was accounted for, as records were incomplete. We asked if the younger woman had been given a power of attorney, and were told that she had not.

Following the interview, after a more thorough check of such records as there were, we did some investigating through our own sources. We became pretty well-convinced that there was not malfeasance, and that the woman handling the accounts was honest but not thoroughly careful enough in keeping records.

When next we talked with the older woman and tried to exonerate her friend, we again asked if she was certain no power of attorney had been given. This time she said, "Oh, my—yes. She has a power of attorney. Of course."

Point one. In appointing someone as attorney-in-fact (as you do under a power of attorney) be sure that person is not only trustworthy but also competent to handle the duties. Handling includes whatever proper record keeping is called for in the given circumstances.

Point two. In accepting appointment under a power of attorney recognize that you may be criticized, justly or unjustly, for your performance. Maintain records, and be prepared at any time to justify your course of action. The job calls for diligence, and it entails very real responsibilities.

There is a bit more to the story. We learned that the older woman had told the younger that when she (the older) died some very good stock would be left to her friend for the services performed and the help given. But when she died a few months later she left a will with no such provision. I imagine that she really had meant to make the bequest, but she just had not gotten around to it. This, I suppose, could be made into another point to the effect of collecting now, not later, if you are to be reimbursed for services rendered under a power of attorney.

The power terminates at the death of the grantor. At that time all future action rests with the executor or administrator.

Gifts

Gifts during life are satisfying to make.

Gifts are pleasant to receive.

Gifts can be of effective use in estate planning.

Gifts can be tax savers.

Gifts can also create problems, bring unexpected tax results, and be regretted because of their finality.

Before we explore some aspects of gifts, let us look at some examples in support of the last statement above.

Gifts can create problems. One friend made a gift of a substantial amount of stock in the family-held company to a son who works in the business. The husband, who made the gift, retained enough stock to keep control and to provide income for his widow should he die before she does.

The problem arose when another son came into the business and father wanted to give him a substantial amount of stock, too. How could that be done if control was to be retained along with protection for a surviving widow? Could the first gift have been premature? Or too large? Whatever the answers, it certainly created a problem.

As to bringing some unexpected tax results, I read of one case in which a man unwittingly made a gift to his wife. When his attorney told him what he had done, the man responded that he would just have his wife agree to undoing it by setting everything back to the way it had been originally. He was shocked when his attorney told him that his proposed course of action would create another gift, this time from wife to husband.

Gifts can be regretted. Perhaps you recall the story in the chapter on trusts of the man who put some property into an irrevocable trust, and then wanted to undo the gift only to find that he could not. True gifts are final.

Size and Consequences of Gifts

If you have no expectation of making gifts, any one of which would exceed $3,000 in value, you may not be interested in reading this section.

If you do think it possible that you may make a gift valued in excess of $3,000 then it would be wise, almost imperative, that you become informed about gifts in even greater depth than the treatment afforded here.

What is said in this chapter has to do with gifts as treated by the federal government. Some states have gift tax laws which, more or less, follow old federal patterns; some have no gift tax statute. Your tax adviser can provide you with specifics.

As was said in connection with the marital deduction, there are numerous technicalities, regulations, and complexities in the matter of gifts. The purpose of the treatment below is to alert the reader to some guidelines and to "run up some red flags." There is no intent that this section be considered definitive.

Gifts under $3,000—make them and forget them unless they involve what is known as a "future interest," i.e., a gift the full enjoyment of which cannot be had until some future time. If you have even some slight doubt about the involvement of a future interest in a gift, talk with your tax adviser before making the gift.

The $3,000 is an *annual exclusion* (need not be reported) for each of any number of gifts. Every year you can give to any number of people gifts of value up to $3,000 each. But if the gift exceeds $3,000 —what then? Read on.

The Unified Credit

The Tax Reform Act of 1976 created a new concept and new set of involved rules for Federal Gift and Estate Taxes.

Each individual now has a *credit* to be applied against Gift and Estate taxes owed. Note that this is a *credit* against tax, not just a deduction. It is being phased in gradually from $30,000 in 1977, reaching its ultimate maximum of $47,000 in 1981.

What the unifying means is that lifetime taxable gifts and estate worth are combined in the final tax and tax credit calculations. Credit is given for gift taxes paid during life.

For example, if in some year you make a gift of $25,000 to some one person, then you have given $22,000 in excess of the $3,000 annual exclusion explained above. Whatever the tax may be on that along with other gifts in excess of $3,000 which you have made, it becomes a part of the total unified tax against which your credit is ultimately applied.

It is all a very complicated and tricky business. The main thing to remember is that if you contemplate making a gift in excess of $3,000 do not consummate it until you have had good professional advice.

The 1976 act also provides for a $100,000 marital deduction for gifts between spouses. Here again, if you plan a gift in excess of $3,000 to your spouse be sure to find out what the impact will be on your final unified tax and your credit. (The government giveth, and the government taketh away.)

One additional caution. If you do make any gift in

excess of $3,000, make certain that you promptly file the necessary Gift Tax forms—even if you are paying no tax therewith.

Advantages of Gifts

Gifts made during life afford not only the satisfaction of giving, but also certainty. Cash is always welcome, but there are other possibilities. The Spode which you never use may be damaged in moving, or a piece or two of it chipped by accident if you retain it until death. The jade bracelet you have always intended for some special person may be lost or stolen by the time you die.

Just this morning I had a discussion in which one woman said, "I never have found out what happened to . . . (certain items) . . . my mother had." What did happen? Who knows?

Gifts of objects, especially of objects rarely used, can be made with gratifying results and to advantage.

Reasons for Handling Gifts with Care

1. It is not unusual for someone to say, "Well, I won't make a gift. I'll just sell that property (of whatever sort) which is worth $10,000 for $2,000." The reasoning is that this will eliminate the making of a gift and perhaps eliminate a capital gains tax if the value really is

now greater than the price originally paid for the property.

But it does not work that way. In the above example there would be a gift of $8,000, the difference between sale price and value.

2. Value? What constitutes value? "Fair market value" is the valuation for tax purposes, i.e., what a willing buyer will pay to a willing seller in a free market. How does one know what this is? Best answer: have an appraisal, or better yet an average of a couple of appraisals by some qualified appraisers.

3. Another little-known trap is the one which is created by the rule that the original cost follows the gift. Example: I pay $2,000 for an antique which once belonged to a famous historical person. A few years later I give it to you. It has increased in value to $3,800. Some time later you give it to your sister. Value: $6,000. A half-dozen years after that she gives it to her daughter. Value then: $10,000. Daughter decides to sell it at fair market value of $10,000. Her reportable gain is the difference between $10,000 and the original cost of $2,000. The person who buys from her, however, will have a base of $10,000 since the acquisition this time was by purchase and not by gift.

4. It is possible to spread gifts over a period of years, keeping each one under $3,000. I know of one case in which the attorney carefully prepares annually a transfer of a small fraction of a piece of property to each of three family

members. Each fraction is valued under $3,000, but over the years each donee has acquired a substantial interest in the property. If the donor lives another few years the entire property will have been transferred. This plan is practical for some gifts but not for others. If used it should be handled by a competent, professional person.

Joint Property

In general it may be said that there are two kinds of joint ownership of property. Tenancy in common is the form under which each joint owner may sell, give, borrow against his or her portion of the property, or dispose of it by will, all without agreement or consent of the other joint holder.

As an example, you and your sister might buy a small apartment house as tenants in common. You could decide later to sell your interest, and your sister then would have a new joint tenant in common with her.

Entirely different is the matter of tenancy by entirety, or tenancy with right of survivorship. This form of ownership between spouses does not allow transfer or loan against the property except by mutual consent. At death of either spouse the property becomes that of the survivor.

It has the advantage of passing directly, outside the probate process, to the surviving spouse. That does not mean that it passes without tax. In some states it does; in some it does not. For federal tax purposes it depends upon a number of factors including: whose money went into the joint property, treatment as a taxable gift at the time of creation of the joint tenancy, and the date of creation. The 1976 law created a "mixed bag" too technical to discuss here. If you own, or contemplate owning joint property with your spouse, or anyone else for that matter, you would do well to consult with your tax adviser to secure counsel as to the taxable status.

Joint property is indeed a "Handle with Care" subject. Its ramifications are rarely understood except by those in professional fields who have occasion to deal with them. Here are a few examples of advantages, disadvantages, and differences in tax treatments among the states.

The sole purpose of giving these few examples is to establish the need for competent counselling before making a commitment to joint ownership of any sort.

One advantage of a tenancy by entirety is readily seen because of the easy passing of the property at death, as stated above.

The offsetting disadvantage is that property held by the entirety or with right of survivorship is not flexible for planning purposes. A year or so ago I talked with a man and wife who owned an estate of about $750,000, almost every bit of which was jointly owned. How does one plan that for estate purposes? Which spouse will die first? Who will eventually own the estate which is left after taxes and costs? How can distribution plans be established with any certainty? One cannot dispose of property held under a tenancy by entirety or with right of survivorship by will.

Some steps can be taken in such an instance but they are fraught with pitfalls along the way, and they may or may not reach the objectives really desired.

Generally, for psychological reasons, if no other, it is desirable for a married couple to own the family home in a tenancy by the entirety. Beyond that, good counsel is advisable before acquiring additional joint property, or disposing of jointly held property.

Not all states allow tenancy in common between spouses.

In four states income from property held in tenancy by the entirety is considered to be the right of the husband.

Putting property into or out of joint tenancy often creates a taxable gift.

Too much property held under tenancy by entirety or with right of survivorship often creates difficulties in planning the estate, and may very well eventuate in unnecessary taxes in the estate of the surviving spouse.

Joint property is like other good things: enough is enough. So wherever you live—whether it be in a community property state or a common law state—handle with care property titling and property transfers.

Contemplating Starting a Business?

Many women want to be in business for themselves, or control their own enterprises. If this is for you, where do you go from there?

1. Objectives. (You have heard that before.) Why do you want to go into your own business? Money? The fun of it? To be your own boss? To render a specific service because of a talent or skill you have? Why? That should be decided first. It will help point your way.

2. Do you have adequate knowledge of the business, any product or service involved, and what the competition will be?

3. Does it require capital? How much? Rule of thumb is that you should have, or at least have ready access to one-third the required capital.

4. Have you made a projection of what you think the business can produce during each of the first three years? Have you really sound reasons for your estimates?

5. Based on what you have made as a three-year projection, have you prepared a budget, including a fair amount for contingencies? Then having looked at what is left after subtracting expenses from in-

come, are you satisfied with that figure as your income?

6. Only after you have done the above are you ready to talk with your banker and with a representative of the Small Business Administration, both of whom you will find helpful. That help may be encouraging or discouraging, but it will be valuable.

7. All things in proper time and order. If you are encouraged after having followed through on the above then it is time for a host of other considerations. What form of business structure: corporation, partnership, or sole proprietorship? Location? Lease? Personnel?, etc., etc. Competent advice will be essential at this stage, but then by this stage you will know a great deal more than when you started out considering point "1" above.

Taxes

Ah, would that a tidy little paragraph or two could provide all necessary information. Before me I have one book on federal income taxes of over 500 pages, and one on estate and gift taxes of over 300 pages.

Perhaps the best that can be done in a volume of this sort is to point out what some of the common taxes are and to mention some records which should be kept in order that you might file properly and at the same time be able to support your deductions if they are challenged.

Here are some of the taxes which any one of us may be exposed to, and for which we may be accountable. The list is not complete, but it does include the ones most likely to be encountered. Not all states and municipalities have all of the taxes listed.

Federal: Income Tax, Gift Tax, Estate Tax.

State: Income Tax, Inheritance or Estate Tax, Personal Property or Intangibles Tax, Gift Tax, Real Estate Transfer Tax.

Municipal: Earned Income Tax, Real Estate Tax, Per Capita Tax, Occupation Tax, School Tax.

Sales taxes and excise taxes usually are collected at time of purchase, so except for purposes of allowable deductions they do not require separate reporting.

It is important to make certain that you are aware of all taxes to which you are subject. Failure to report can mean big trouble. I had a friend who was completely unaware that the state where he lived imposed an intangibles tax. For several years he filed no returns, not knowing any were due. Then the state taxing authorities caught up with him. He had to pay not only the taxes, but interest and penalties as well.

If you are not positive about what taxes apply to you, by all means consult your tax adviser.

Records

Keeping records of income and expenses is important enough just for checking actual financial performance against budget. In addition to that reason, however, there is the very important one of the need for various records when it is time to prepare an income tax return.

Items such as taxes paid, medical expenses, casualty losses, and contributions made to church and charities are important ones. Keeping record of them as they are incurred can save hours when you are working on that annual chore of preparing your income tax return.

Retention of Records

The question of how long records should be retained often arises. Here are some suggested indications with comments. It will be seen that in some situations it becomes a judgmental matter. A few general guidelines may be helpful, however, as they relate to frequently held records.

First of all, there is a group of records which should be kept indefinitely: birth certificate, marriage certificate, will, trust, certain military papers such as discharge and certification of disability, Social Security card along with any special correspondence such as that pertaining to a dispute regarding average monthly earnings, benefits, etc., and real estate papers.

The matter of real estate papers is a sort of "It depends" classification, so better practice dictates erring, if there is to be erring, on the side of indefinite retention.

If the only real estate you ever owned was an inherited mountain lot which you sold more than three years ago (see next section), you are probably perfectly safe in destroying the papers. After all, there are records at the courthouse.

But if you owned a residence, sold it, reinvested the money in a more expensive home—and possibly did the same another time or so, then it would be wise to keep all those records including those of improvements made. If in doubt keep the records.

In addition to the records on the above list there may be certain others, as will be pointed out in subsequent paragraphs.

For Internal Revenue Service purposes the records used in preparation of an income tax return and, therefore, the information which would be supporting information for the taxpayer if a question were to be raised about a return, should be kept for three years. That really means three full tax years. (A record supporting a deduction taken as being incurred in December of this year would be only two years and some days old at the outset of the third calendar year hence.)

In this group of records would be included: check and other bank statements, those receipts pertinent to supporting your entries on income tax forms, notes, sales contracts, etc. on which final payment has been made. Records of some transactions involving securities could also be included, but others should be retained longer. Here again, "It depends."

If you buy a listed stock, sell it a year later, report your gain or loss, then the three years is probably long enough to keep the records.

But if you have a bond which runs for 15 years, and during that time some of the principal has been paid out, or if you have stock in a company which in some years has indicated that part of your dividend represents a return of capital, or if you had stock in a company which even after three years is still in the process of liquidation, you should keep the various information records. Again, if you are in doubt retain the records.

In addition to the above, all pertinent records should be retained for any transactions or claim which is in dispute, or which you anticipate may eventuate in dispute or possible litigation. Statutes of limitations vary among the states, so how long pertinent records should be kept is also a variable.

Before "cleaning house" with receipts, it is a good rule to ask yourself about each one, "Might I ever need this?"

Final Potpourri

Procrastination is the evil genie of financial and estate planning.

———————

Assuming and misunderstanding are the assistant devils.

———————

Failure to update wills and beneficiary arrangements for insurance policies is exactly like giving money to people for whom it was not intended.

———————

There are two sources of income for you: you at work and your money at work. If your money is not working it does not draw any unemployment benefits.

———————

There is a third certainty in addition to taxes and death—change. We have to meet and accept the first two. Why should we not prepare to do the same with the third?

––––––––––––

"You can't take it with you," but that is no reason for leaving it in a mess.

––––––––––––

The distance from objective to achievement is measured in steps.

––––––––––––

When you know that you know not, hark to those words from the Book of Proverbs: "Hear counsel, and receive instruction, that thou mayest be wise——."

Questions on Chapter Nine

1. Have you made inquiry as to the laws governing access to a safe deposit box after death of a holder in your state?

2. Could you describe to a friend the purpose of a power of attorney? The difference between a limited and a general power?

3. What are some considerations before granting or accepting a power of attorney?

4. What is the difference between tenancy by the entirety and tenancy in common?

5. What are some advantages and disadvantages of tenancy by the entirety?

6. What rights do you retain under a tenancy in common?

7. Why make gifts? Especially gifts valued at less than $3,000? Why not wait to make bequests of the items?

8. Could you explain to a friend the unified tax and the unified credit for gift and estate purposes?

9. If you were considering going into your own business what are some steps you should take before finalizing anything?

10. Do you know for sure all of the taxes for which you are, or may be liable?

11. Which of the Potpourri ingredients means the most to you? Why?

Index

204 What Every Woman Should Know About Finances

CHOLESTEROL CONTROL
COOKERY   (03795-9—$1.75)
   by Dorothy Revell

DR. SOLOMON'S PROVEN   (03620-0—$2.25)
MASTER PLAN FOR
TOTAL BODY FITNESS
AND BODY MAINTENANCE

FAST HEALTH   (03460-2—$1.75)
   By Joseph Pilcher

THE FIBER FACTOR   (03460-7—$1.50)
   by Anne Moyer and the
   editors of PREVENTION

FOREVER THIN   (04044-5—$1.75)
   Theodore Isaac Rubin

GROWING UP THIN   (03169-1—$1.50)
   By Alvin N. Eden with
   Joan Rattner Heilman

HEALTH, YOUTH AND BEAUTY   (03792-4—$1.50)
THROUGH COLOR BREATHING
   by Linda Clark and
   Yvonne Martine

THE NEW DIET DOES IT   (03567-0—$1.75)
   by Gayelord Hauser

Send for a list of all our books in print.

These books are available at your local bookstore, or send price indicated plus 30¢ for postage and handling. If more than four books are ordered, only $1.00 is necessary for postage. Allow three weeks for delivery. Send orders to:

   Berkley Book Mailing Service
   P.O. Box 690
   Rockville Centre, New York 11570

Sit down, relax and read a good book...

CURRENT BESTSELLERS FROM BERKLEY

THE BOOK OF MERLYN   (03826-2—$2.25)
    by T. H. White

THE SECOND DEADLY SIN   (03923-4—$2.50)
    by Lawrence Sanders

BLUEPRINT   (03876-9—$2.25)
    by Philippe Van Rjndt

THE LAST CONVERTIBLE   (04034-8—$2.50)
    by Anton Myrer

NINE AND A HALF WEEKS   (04032-1—$2.25)
    by Elizabeth McNeill

MY SEARCH FOR   (04011-9—$1.95)
THE GHOST OF FLIGHT 401
    by Elizabeth Fuller

THE POISON THAT FELL   (04013-5—$2.25)
FROM THE SKY
    by John G. Fuller

DUNE   (03698-7—$2.25)
    by Frank Herbert

Send for a list of all our books in print.

These books are available at your local bookstore, or send price indicated plus 30¢ for postage and handling. If more than four books are ordered, only $1.00 is necessary for postage. Allow three weeks for delivery. Send orders to:

      Berkley Book Mailing Serice
      P.O. Box 690
      Rockville Centre, New York 11570